◀ LODER'S WHITE

DEXTER HYBRID
Hampfler Studios

RHODODENDRONS IN AMERICA

Ted Van Veen

LORD ROBERTS

Binford & Mort Publishing

Portland, Oregon

LAVENDER GIRL

RHODODENDRONS IN AMERICA

Printed in the United States of America
Library of Congress Catalog Number: 77-104390
ISBN: 0-8323-0374-7 (softcover)
ISBN: 0-8323-0450-6 (hardcover)

First Edition 1969
First Edition, Second Printing 1976
Japanese Printing 1976
Second Edition 1980
Second Edition, Second Printing 1986

DEDICATED TO

...the explorers and hybridists who are responsible for the wide array of rhododendrons in our landscape today, I gratefully dedicate this book. Gardening horizons throughout the world have been broadened by the courageous and patient efforts of these remarkable people. Particularly, I wish to honor three hybridists of exceptional and affectionate interest to me, whose developments have created an unprecedented enthusiasm for rhododendrons ...
A. M. Shammarello, Joseph B. Gable and, my father, Theodore Van Veen.

VAN VEEN

Introduction

Rhododendrons are beautifully interwoven with my earliest memories. You see, my father was an expert in growing these lovely, colorful plants. I am sure he was an expert mainly because he loved rhododendrons. I love them too. My affection for rhododendrons is surpassed only by love for my family. I hope, in the pages of this book, to tell you why I feel this way.

"Rhodies," as they are affectionately nicknamed, are almost always more than just plants to the gardener; they are part of his family. Their blooms tell of spring more magnificently than other plants. Their handsome, lush foliage enriches the exterior of any home where rhododendrons are used, no matter what the season. In addition, when winter's chilly call is at hand, the person who loves rhododendrons finds empathy with the plants as they hang their leaves in protest.

One might believe that because I grew up surrounded by rhododendrons, I might think them to be commonplace. Who could ever consider a rhododendron commonplace? They are as regal as Queen Victoria, whose homeland contributed so much to the development of rhododendrons.

It is my sincere wish, through this book, to share with you my impressions and knowledge of rhododendrons, spanning the years from boyhood to present. I want to tell those of you, who may not be familiar with rhododendrons, why you should learn more about these plants and why you should grow them in your garden. I wish to relay to you, who are already close friends of the rhododendron, my ideas for their use and care in the landscape. I hope that some of my thoughts will help you produce rhodies that are the talk of the town!

Perhaps most important, I would like to convince many of you who may feel "left out" that you can grow rhododendrons in your climate. With careful moisture control, sufficient light, mulching and proper protection, some species and various new hybrids can be grown in rather rugged parts of the country. An oasis of climate can be created artificially in warm, arid places, making possible the use of rhododendrons. You *can* join the increasing number of rhododendron enthusiasts.

As you read through this informative book and gaze at its many beautiful full-color pictures of rhododendrons, I believe you will enjoy it; learn much from it; and that like me, you will develop a true love for rhododendrons.

A small boy playing among the rhododendrons may have been more impressed by the "swell hideout" they provided for him rather than their beauty. Today, I believe that man, soon capable of visiting distant planets, will find nothing in plant life there to exceed the beauty of our rhododendrons right here on earth.

AMERICA

Contents

ANTOON van WELIE

Foreword

The cultivation of rhododendrons in large numbers is a recent development in the United States, as such things go in horticultural history. For nearly three-quarters of a century, their charisma was created by a general association with high cost, great estates and the esoteric indulgences of the wealthy.

The advent of the affluent society, vast improvements in propagation methods and the proliferation of new hybrids resulting from the startling discoveries of the turn-of-the-century plant explorers have combined to produce a population explosion in rhododendrons. Several decades ago the choices of hybrids from nurserymen for garden planting numbered in the dozens. Now a fervent and persistent collector in a mild climate should easily be able to assemble a thousand different hybrids. The burgeoning field has escaped the general gardener to become the province of the specialist.

So it is a very real service to horticulture when a veteran professional grower of rhododendrons selects the best for general garden planting out of the myriad hybrids produced since 1900, and presents them graphically. The experienced specialist distills his knowledge to restore a vast field to the general gardener's ken.

Here at last, then, in *Rhododendrons in America* we have a picture book of the best garden rhododendrons, and in living color, too. But the phrase is no promotional cliche as applied to publications on rhododendrons. To this day, less than half a dozen books on rhododendrons have been produced in this country. Never before have we had one devoted to lavish illustration. It is an occasion for rejoicing that a group of plants so specialized should receive such opulent largesse from author and publisher.

How does the eager amateur visualize the "red" or "medium pink" or "lavender blue" of the nurseryman's list? Vernacular color descriptions leave only a carbon smudge of the reality. There is no communication of the charm of subtle color gradations, of the elegance—or lack of it—with which the flowers are presented, of the aesthetically important scale of the blossoms in relation to the size of the leaves and branches. A "red" rhododendron can be of great character and distinction or it can be a pedestrian plebe.

And here, of course, is the unique value of this book. The professional nurseryman can show his customers exactly what floral qualities they can expect from the hybrids he offers. The landscape architect can instrument his colors with precision for harmony or contrast. The uninitiated amateur can decide in advance exactly which rhododendrons enthrall him, and then go out to buy them with the comforting knowledge that he is not an innocent sailor afloat on a sea of commercial exploitations. The quality and hardiness ratings for over 300 cultivars popular in commerce will save many a gardener his dollars and his frustrations.

Rhododendrons in America is not intended for the botanist, the phylogenist, the entomologist or any academic "ist". It is an intensely practical book which lays no claim to being a comprehensive treatment of the genus. Ted Van Veen, the largest commercial grower of rhododendrons in the United States, exuberantly summarizes the selection, uses, planting and cultivation of rhododendrons according to his cheerfully admitted preferences and prejudices. His informal narrative includes such personal hang-ups as how to dispose of a used insecticide container; a warning not to use DDT because of its extended half-life in the biosphere; how to take a soil sample; and how to build a compost pile. The text is larded with homely tips for the amateur novice and ruminations dear to the author's heart. The whole is a clear reflection of a man who loves rhododendrons, is luxuriously contended with his trade and is eager to share his fulfillment with others.

David G. Leach

Brookville, Pa.
September 9, 1969

XI

PILGRIM

KING TUT

CHAPTER ONE

From Whence Rhododendrons?

 If I were to tell you that rhododendrons encircle the globe, would you believe me? And if I said that one species, *R. lapponicum*, literally surrounds the North Pole region, would that seem logical? Would those of you who are accustomed to growing the "traditional" rhododendrons in your garden, using soil replete with organic matter and supplying a cool root area, believe that another species, *R. chapmanii*, thrives in the sand dunes of Florida? These statements are true! No wonder we need not fear to try growing certain rhododendrons under various hardiness and climatic hazards, for there are varieties suited to many unusual environments. All that is required in most instances, is some basic knowledge of the culture for the general line of rhododendrons grown commercially, and then the determination to provide the necessary growing conditions which seem logical for those varieties you select. Lest I mislead you, there are many parts of North America where rhododendrons are not native. However, most of these areas certainly can become adopted homes for these crown jewels of the garden.

Before I go any further, I would like to clarify that, primarily, this book is written about that large segment of the genus *Rhododendron* which we commonly call "rhododendrons" and not about the *Azalea,* which also is of the genus *Rhododendron.* A possible exception to that rule is the matter of background discussed in this chapter. Also, most of the cultural matters pertaining to rhododendrons apply equally to azaleas. There are about 1,000 basic species of the genus *Rhododendron,* including some 70 azaleas.

I believe most home gardeners better understand the term "species" rather than "cultivar" or "clone." Throughout this book it is my intention to make use of the more common word "variety" when referring to hybrids.

WHERE THEY GROW

One of my favorite boasts about Oregon and the Pacific Northwest, including Northern California and British Columbia, is that it is one area in North America where native rhododendrons grow in abundance. When the native species are in bloom during late spring and early summer, I love to journey to the Mt. Hood area or along the Pacific Coast Range where the woods are bright with the beauty of *R. macrophyllum.* Another Northwest native seen as far east as Colorado is *R. albiflorum.* And I must mention the Oregon azalea, *R. occidentale,* which abounds in the Pacific Northwest.

The mountains and seaboard of the eastern United States have their counterparts in three fine species that grow in the Blue Ridge Mountains of the Southeast; another grows from that same area as far north as

VIRGINIA RICHARDS, *one of Bill Whitney's exciting new hybrids. A wonderful all-year plant because of the superb foliage. There is another form in the trade with more pink in the flower.*

the New England States, even into Maine and Quebec. The first three mentioned are *R. carolinianum*, *R. minus* and *R. catawbiense*. The other, extending into the north, is *R. maximum* or Rose Bay. *R. catawbiense* grows at elevations as high as 6,000 feet in full sun, thanks to cooling breezes and rainfall factors. Several other species rhododendrons are found in the southeastern United States.

Native rhododendrons in Europe are few. *R. ferrugineum* (Alpine Rose) is one found with several others in the high mountains of Europe. For some reason, *ferrugineum* never has been a popular landscape species. On the other hand, sometimes a rhododendron, like other native plants, will find an adopted home very much to its liking and become naturalized, literally escaping the cultured boundaries of the landscape. One of the most outstanding examples is *R. ponticum*. I believe that even some of the English consider this species native to their homeland where it covers large areas, although it originally came from Asia Minor and southeastern Europe.

It is Asia to which we are indebted for the great majority of our rhododendrons, especially those species which in themselves are popular as landscape plants, or those from which our finest hybrids have been developed. The number of important species coming to us from the Orient is legion. The Himalayan region's lower mountains and foothills form the main natural growing area for rhododendrons, particularly in western China and northern India. Many species are found in Assam, Burma and southern and southeastern China. Japan, the Marshall Islands and Okinawa, and other Asian localities also produce native rhododendrons.

In Indonesia, Malaya and Cambodia are found the "Javanicum" rhododendrons. While some are epiphytic and quite tender, there are many other species found in the snow fields of alpine regions. Like so many of the species, it could well be that these rhododendrons some day may provide the basis of a breeding program that will produce an entirely new form, acceptable for landscaping in colder climates.

A. BEDFORD, *a lavender jewel for any garden setting. Best tall, large-leaved "blue." Use in a background planting.*

Here I would like to pause to pay tribute to the botanical explorers who first sought out the early rhododendrons. Without the ambition, endurance and patience of these pioneers, we simply would not have all the rhododendron beauty we enjoy today. They are high on my list of great contributors to our culture.

Other than native North American species of rhododendrons, this country was not the first stop for imported species. They went primarily to England, and later some were taken to Germany, France, Holland and several other European countries. Famous names in horticulture such as Loder and Rothschild, have been associated with these "exotics." Because of the wealth of these prominent men, it was natural that they would import rhododendrons and develop them. A hobby of this kind was costly and time consuming.

It is interesting to me that so much Japanese history is associated with azaleas and rhododendrons. In one section of that country, growers jealously guard their ex-clusive variation of a species. For another grower or gardener to see or endeavor to collect all (some 250 variations), would require an individual call on each grower. Those facts mentioned earlier concerning the wide variances of rhododendron species native to America and the conditions under which they grow are true of other areas also. In Japan, for instance, rhododendron species found in the southern island grow in dry situations. *R. japonicum (Azalea japonica)*, which grows in the northern area, is found in bogs. Incidentally, it is interesting to note that the yellow azalea colors abound in the southern island of Japan, but proceeding northward into the colder climate, they become less plentiful. In other words, yellow colors are not native to colder climates, but the red azaleas seem to thrive there.

CLASSIFYING THE NATIVES

The system of classifying native rhododendrons is intensely interesting and quite intricate. A knowledge is required of colors, shapes, habits, and foliage shapes and sizes. The matter of classification goes so far as to

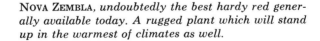

NOVA ZEMBLA, *undoubtedly the best hardy red generally available today. A rugged plant which will stand up in the warmest of climates as well.*

include plant hairs to be certain of identification. Today there exists in Washington, D.C., data on more than 8,000 specimens of native plants. Computers have long been used in the identification of rhododendrons, for each specimen has its own computerized data which includes some 80 characteristics.

Earliness of bloom and hardiness are of particular interest in the breeding of rhododendrons, for they help to determine what can be expected of plants bred from certain parents. The "expected" does not always occur, however, because the tendencies of one parent may overcome those of the other, and because some parent species cover widespread climatic situations.

The international scope of rhododendrons, and the fraternal feeling that exists between those who love these magnificent plants often come to mind. These aspects were impressed upon me most vividly in 1961 when I attended the International Rhododendron Conference in Portland, Oregon, and heard the world's foremost experts of rhododendron culture speak and exchange their ideas freely. All were interested in further developing rhododendron culture, which

Don Gray

CATAWBIENSE GRANDIFLORUM, *a good background plant with a habit similar to 'Roseum Elegans'. The flowers hold up well over a long blooming period.*

CHEER, *and cheer it will bring to any garden, for cheerful it is. A free flowering Shammarello hybrid. Good reports of successful performance from many of the more difficult growing areas in the Midwest.*

VAN NES SENSATION, *overhead shade will better bring out the delicate coloring of the pleasantly fragrant flowers. R. maximum parentage helps it grow well in the very hot climates. Notice the seven lobes on the flowers.*

would make it possible to use rhododendrons in every conceivable situation of the landscape. A good example is the work reported by Herr Dietrich Hobbie, telling of his successful efforts, through hybridization, to produce rhododendrons capable of surviving subzero temperatures, and of his work in producing calcium-tolerant varieties. The climatic situation Herr Hobbie is dealing with in Linswege, Oldenberge, Germany, is in sharp contrast to that found in my home state of Oregon with its even temperatures and ample rainfall. Yet he showed us color slides of magnificent century-old rhododendrons growing in Linswege!

Closer to home, it was interesting for me to learn from P.H. Brydon, while he was curator of the famed Strybing Arboretum, that rhododendrons were not introduced to the San Francisco area until 1915. Now they almost seem native there.

BACKGROUND OF PROPAGATION

Although I do not intend to deal with propagation, per se, in this book, believing that it is a topic mainly of interest to commercial producers of rhododendrons and to plant breeders, there are some interesting facts about propagation that I think you would enjoy learning.

PEEKABOO, *hanging bells seem ready to peal of their charm. An interesting dwarf for the rockery which has a little different foliage than the usual red R. repens types.*

Ever since the mid-nineteenth century, the propagation of rhododendrons has been studied from both commercial and scientific viewpoints. Investigations through the years led to considerable controversy over the best procedures for layerage, graftage and cuttage. My own father was among the earliest to experiment with cuttings on a commercial basis. Some of his findings were that hard-to-root varieties have sensitive stems which must be wounded in order for the cutting to root properly, and that these difficult ones need maximum leaf area since leaf efficiency is low. The terminal leaf bud is inhibitory and must be removed. Dad's work with rhododendron propagation was among the first serious efforts along this line, dating back to the mid-30's. I believe he was in the forefront with his research, using misting and lead-cable bottom heat, paving the way for future efforts by others in this important work.

What do I think is in store for rhododendrons in the future? One thing is certain.

Since China's doors are closed to plant explorers and other troubles exist in prime areas of search for native rhododendrons, I doubt very much if any significant exploration will take place for a considerable time. I believe there are more species of rhododendrons, and certainly variations of species, awaiting discovery by plantsmen at a later, more peaceful time. Until then, we will continue to breed new plants, using known species. There is much "magic" yet to be performed. Modern procedures make it possible to store pollen. Anthers are collected, dried and placed in capsules which, in turn, go into well-sealed jars containing a small amount of calcium dichloride. If you are on good terms with your local druggist, he may give you some of the more convenient small bags which are bottled with certain medicines to absorb moisture. Pollen and anthers are

PURPUREUM ELEGANS, *listed as purple in the official description, it appears to be closer to a blue. A good background plant which seems to be able to take sun.*

Don Gray

FAGGETTER'S FAVOURITE, *a rhapsody in color with scar-*
let bud, and the open flower with blends of pink, cream
and lavender. Will flower too heavily at times so it is
wise to remove some of the buds. Flowers and foliage
are best out of the hot sun.

frozen and can be refrozen repeatedly between usages as crosses are made with flowers of rhododendrons that bloom at different
times. The list of possibilities is endless,
considering the ever-increasing number of
hybrids being introduced.

It is a foregone conclusion that rhododendrons will be in greater use in the landscape.
How can it be otherwise? People throughout
the country are becoming aware of the fact
that rhododendrons can be used almost any
place, if the proper plants are selected and
given the attention required for each particular environment.

MRS. FURNIVAL, *a near perfect rhododendron in every*
way. 'Loder's White' is the only other hybrid which
the American Rhododendron Society has given top
rating for both flower and plant. Holds up well in
warm weather and is hardy to a temperature of 10
below zero.

CHAPTER TWO

Let's Landscape
With Rhododendrons

 One of the rhododendron's most gratifying attributes is its longevity. Owner and plant can live out their lives together. What other plant can provide so much breath-taking beauty when in bloom and such quieting, majestic grandeur of foliage and form, along with perpetuity?

Brian O. Mulligan, Director of the University of Washington Arboretum in Seattle, Washington, once sent a questionnaire to rhododendron growers in the Pacific Northwest, seeking information concerning the types of soil, exposure, climatic conditions and other factors pertaining to the use of rhododendrons in the landscape. As to soils, he learned that gardeners were growing rhododendrons with success in clay, heavy clay, clay with peat and sand added, sandy soil, stony well-drained soil, a combination of sand and gravel with much humus added, sandy soil plus humus, coarse gravelly soil, and sandy alluvial soils.

The sites also varied widely. Rhododendrons were planted in cold positions, cold and windy, northeast exposure, western exposure, sunny situations, southern exposure, near salt water, in the mountains and numerous other combinations of these situations. The gardeners reporting stated that plants with ages of 20, 25, 28, 29, 30, 34, 35, 38, 40 and up to 44 years were still going strong!

Soil selection and exposure depend upon various factors. An imporant consideration is that often one variety will accept conditions totally unacceptable to another variety. In later chapters, I explain how to cope with climatic factors, exposure and soil. I think you will be amazed by the success that is possible, regardless of where you live.

RHODODENDRONS BELONG

There are rhododendrons of all sizes, making it possible to use them in almost any landscaping situation. I already have referred briefly to the large ones, some attaining heights of twenty feet or more, if given time and ideal growing conditions. Most popular, I believe, are those of medium height, the semi-dwarfs and the dwarf or miniature rhododendrons. Modern homes generally dictate the use of small to medium height plants. Gardeners blessed with a home in a wooded setting or surrounded by spacious grounds can utilize the larger forms. One could not behold a more magnificent display of nature's beauty in the spring than that supplied by a banking of rhododendrons, ranging from the miniatures in a border to the giants in the background.

The dwarf varieties provide plants for many garden situations as, for instance, a ground cover or border and in the rockery. Used as a ground cover, they are unsurpassed. These miniatures require little care, making them especially popular with the

BOW BELLS, *how better to frame a picture window? A top quality landscape plant in which the dense growth is full to the ground. Typical of R. williamsianum hybrids, the foliage on new growth is copper bronze. Does best with slight shade.*

week-end gardeners. In addition, the dwarf forms are well adapted to the low, rambling type of home built today. Another attraction is the diversity of foliage among the dwarf varieties.

In defense of those of us who produce rhododendrons commercially, I would like to explain the reason for the inadequate collection of dwarf rhododendrons that sometimes is found in garden centers or retail nurseries. It is not because there is a dearth of varieties, since there are many fine dwarfs. The American public, so accustomed to thinking in terms of the "giant economy size," unfortunately often applies the same theory to plants. The consumer feels that a plant in a small-size category should sell for

less money. This logic holds true when one is thinking about a small-size plant which will grow much larger. But the production cost of a naturally smaller dwarf and a normally large plant is almost the same.

There is a bonus benefit derived from the use of rhododendron miniatures, as they can extend the blooming season by months. Since I am so enthusiastic about the use of rhododendrons in the landscape, I want you to enjoy their floral beauty for the longest possible time. During a normal winter in the Pacific Northwest, these delightful little fellows start to flower in late January or early February.

The name "rhododendron" is appropriate for these outstanding plants. It is the Greek word for "tree rose." So, misleading as the translation may seem, it denotes the majesty associated with rhododendrons and roses. I believe that the rhododendron, an evergreen plant that thrives with simple care, is the popular choice.

Consider the glory that has been attached to rhododendrons. The tenacity which we ascribe to England is epitomized by the use of rhododendrons in the landscape of its lovely old gardens. The treasure-trove of rhododendrons in English gardens dates back to the early 1840's when some of the existing plants were first grown. They have outlasted generations of gardeners who occupied the palatial estates. No wonder the English love rhododendrons! They truly are part of the families that have cared for and enjoyed them for nearly a century and a half.

We have some venerable old plants here in the United States, too. Rhododendrons were a part of the floral beauty exhibited in Philadelphia at the Centennial Exposition honoring the anniversary of our Declaration of Independence. Planted there permanently, still flourishing and blooming annually, they have become thrilling reminders of the glory of that event.

RHODODENDRONS ARE FOR YOU

At this point, are you wondering if it is possible to grow rhododendrons in your landscape? Do you live in Quebec or in Michigan, Indiana, Georgia, Texas, California, in some of the other continental states or in the provinces of Canada? Then I can assure you that you can grow beautiful rhododendrons, although perhaps not all varieties, but at least enough for you to become another enthusiastic fan of these lovely plants.

Admittedly, the enthusiasm for rhododendrons runs very high in the Pacific Northwest. This is due in part to perfect climatic conditions making it possible to grow almost all types of rhododendrons. No doubt, this is the reason so many rhododendron buffs are congregated in Oregon and Washington.

It is logical, then, that a number of these rhododendron enthusiasts would meet in 1944 to formulate plans for the American Rhododendron Society, which was incorporated under Oregon law in 1945. There may be a chapter of the ARS near you, a source of valuable information on rhododendron culture exclusive to your area.

The chapters of the American Rhododendron Society, each with some members who are experts and some down-to-earth rhodo-

MRS. E. C. STIRLING, *an obviously excellent grower in full sun. Very floriferous with interesting stages of pink coloring from bud to fade out.*

dendron gardeners, are: Albany-Mohawk, New York; Azalea, Southeast; California; Connecticut; Eugene, Oregon; Grays Harbor, Washington; Great Lakes; Indianapolis; Middle Atlantic; Midwest; New Jersey; New York; North Kitsap, Washington; Olympia, Washington; Olympic Peninsula, Washington; Philadelphia; Portland, Oregon; Princeton, New Jersey; Seattle, Washington; Shelton, Washington; Southeastern, Carolinas; Southern; Tacoma, Washington; Tappan Zee, New York; Tualatin Valley, Oregon; Valley Forge, Pennsylvania; Vancouver, British Columbia. Other chapters are formed as interest dictates.

I mentioned the different situations under which rhododendrons are grown in the Pacific Northwest. Even here, some of our success is possible because of compromises and amendments. Before planting a rhododendron, be certain the site has excellent drainage. The soil around your plants must never become waterlogged. It must be acid and have the proper texture. Special information on soil and handling of the different types is discussed in a later chapter. It is sufficient to say here that the rhododendron root system must have extraordinary aeration and this demands a loose, porous soil, rich in humus.

Many varieties of rhododendrons can be grown in the Pacific Northwest, west of the Cascade Mountain Range, in full open sunlight. Many more varieties perform better with some shade. In the Midwest, where summer humidity is low and temperatures are warm, about 50% shade is required for rhododendrons. Surprisingly, some protection from the winter sun is necessary in the northeastern states and other areas where winters are very cold and winds are drying. Winter winds can draw the moisture right out of a rhododendron that is not properly protected from the sun.

VULCAN, *one of the best garden varieties for general use in all but the coldest of climates. Excellent plant habit in spite of its R. griersonianum blood. There are several different clones in commerce. Resents too much fertilizer.*

PINK TWINS, *ruffled, rapturous, sensational! A hardy hose-in-hose flower on a hybrid which Mr. Gable originally named 'Cathaem #4'. The plant will eventually grow broader than high.*

The gardener living in a hot dry climate has a bit more to consider than a gardener with less stringent weather conditions, but the problems are not in the least insurmountable. He must guard against sun intensity with greater protection from its rays, for high leaf-surface temperatures will encourage fungi growth. It would be best to plant in October and November, so that the rhododendrons can become well established during the winter and spring before hot weather arrives. In the fall, any damaged roots will be less susceptible to disease, which enters easily into wounded root systems when the soil is warm and the plant's energy is being consumed by adjustment to a new home.

In other parts of the country, rhododendrons can be placed in the garden any time in the spring, even when in bloom. Planting should halt, however, during the time of the new fresh growth after flowering. An exception to this rule is in the case of plants in containers. They can be set in the garden at almost any time. A second planting period for balled plants is during months of August and September.

SHADE NEEDS

If you are looking for some sort of indicator that will make it easier to judge the amount of shade required by a particular rhododendron, examine its foliage. The larger the leaf, the more shade required.

Nature is very wise in providing those plants which are sheltered by other plants with greater leaf surface to capture more of the lifegiving rays of the sun. Hence, it is reasonable that plants with large leaves could not possibly receive a heavy bombardment of sun rays without suffering some damage.

Rhododendrons do well in our country along the Gulf of Mexico if they are shaded during the summertime from 9:30 A.M. until late afternoon. In areas comparable to the Piedmont Plateau east of the Blue Ridge Mountains in North Carolina where the altitude runs between 500 to 1000 feet, from 50 to 60 percent shade is required during the summer months. In the Pacific Northwest, I find that most varieties look their best if they have about one-third shade when the sun is warm. The shading of rhododendrons, regardless of the amount of shade provided, is important during the months of June, July and August because new growth is underway at that time. When that new growth is established, the plants can withstand more sun. There is an exception, as I have mentioned, when the winter's sun and wind can take their toll. In fact, more damage is done to rhododendron foliage by drying winter winds than any other cause.

For you who garden in areas like Houston, Texas, I wish to emphasize one point regarding direct sunlight. Even in the evening, plants should be shaded from all except passing glimpses of the sun through the parted leaves of protecting trees. In Houston and similar areas, some rhododendrons will need complete shade. *R. maximum* is a good example. *R. catawbiense*, from which many of our hybrids have been developed, will stand only fleeting sun, even during the morning. Exposed plants develop sun scalds that spoil their appearance. I would recommend 'Nova Zembla', 'Mrs. T. H. Lowinsky' and 'Roseum Elegans' for the Gulf area.

ALBUM ELEGANS, *a tall grower of extreme hardiness for use in a background, or as a color break in a mass rhododendron planting. Flowers open mauve and quickly fade to white.*

SOUVENIR OF W. C. SLOCOCK, *truly a keepsake for the landscape. Will do best in slight shade which will prolong the apricot color of the opening florets.*

Fortunately, in parts of the country where protection from the sun is mandatory, landscaping can be planned around many native trees to excellent advantage. Pines and oaks are excellent cover. It may be necessary to move in some trees noted for shading qualities. It is important, though, that rhododendrons placed near heavy-rooted trees, receive special attention. The competition between tree and rhododendron can be great and, without help, the rhododendron may be the "loser." If native trees exist in the landscape, place rhododendrons in built-up beds in locations most advantageously shaded by the trees. Container plants in large urns or sturdy planters that can be moved about may be the solution. Or, if you feel that it will be adequate help, provide the plants around trees with extra care: More water than ordinarily given (with adequate drainage, of course), a little larger portion of fertilizer, and additional mulching. All these subjects are covered in detail later in this book. Species and hybrids for specific areas are also discussed at length.

LITTLE BERT, *an ideal rock garden shrublet. More amenable to cultivation than its parent, R. repens, but needs more than normal drainage.*

OLD COPPER, *well named because the copper color enriches the handsome bells. Exceptionally good plant habit for a variety with so much R. griersonianum blood. Takes the sun well and has a good record in the warm South.*

ANNIE DALTON, *has received the Award of Excellence. Joe Gable frequently used the beginning syllables of the parents to name new varieties. He originally called this 'Degram', (R. decorum x R. griersonianum) x 'America'.*

DORA AMATEIS, *a spreading, heavy-flowered white with fetching green spots. Even without flowers this is a beautiful, hardy semi-dwarf. The foliage is pleasingly aromatic. 'Dora Amateis' is an interesting cross between our native R. carolinianum and the Asian species, R. ciliatum. Breeders had attempted this mating for years with no success until this breakthrough by Edmond Amateis.*

FOR UNUSUAL SITUATIONS

There are some planting situations you should avoid, especially where weather and other cultural factors may have an adverse influence. The roots of rhododendrons used in a foundation planting or otherwise close to concrete, such as beside a patio or terrace, will reach out and eventually touch the cement. When this occurs, they will absorb too much calcium hydroxide and this will deter normal growth, perhaps even destroy the plants if the soil already is less acid than required by rhododendrons. If you have rhododendrons planted in this type of situation, I suggest that once a year you take a sharp-bladed spade and cut the roots of the plant about one foot from the concrete. Or you can use heavy amounts of iron sulphate and sulphur in the soil next to the concrete (not all around the plant). Then as the calcium leeches out of the cement, it will change to calcium sulfate (gypsum) which is harmless to rhododendrons and other acid-loving plants. When putting in a new planting, I think it best to place heavy pieces of sheet

iron between the plant and the concrete. These should extend about six inches below the foundation or other cemented area. No harm will be done if the roots touch the sheet iron.

It is easier to establish young plants in the landscape rather than to try to move in large plants, unless they are out of containers. Any large plant used must have an adequate root ball or the risk involved in transplanting is increased. For instance, a rhododendron 30 inches tall should have an 18 inch ball for planting in a hot climate and not too much smaller than 18 inches for planting elsewhere. Using plants that are too small also has some risks. It takes them longer to become established, and during that period they are more susceptible to disease and are less hardy than a larger plant.

BLUE PETER, *sharp color contrast always draws comments. There are 15 florets to a truss. Try this variety for cut flowers. While the foliage is most attractive, it is of thin texture which is easily damaged and well liked by chewing insects. Grows equally well in sun or shade.*

BLUE DIAMOND *and* UNIQUE, *how could these have been better named? This color combination is most suitable in areas calling for low plantings. Blue Diamond will take heavy clipping and will make an excellent formal hedge. Although it is a small-leaved variety which does best in the sun, slight shade will bring out the color better.*

Where a soil is heavy, I suggest that you plant rhododendrons "above board." A hole dug in heavy soil will act like a cistern, collecting water and drowning the plant or, at best, cause too much wetness and lead to root rot. Instead, smooth off a space at least five feet in diameter for each rhododendron. Add about two inches of a loose planting medium; I like a 50/50 mixture of peat moss and perlite, without true soil. Build the center of the planting location slightly higher to improve drainage. (Check Chapters V, VII and VIII for information about improving drainage of clay-type soil, providing acidity amendments and protecting from pests at planting time.) The root ball is placed on the peat-perlite mixture and enough of the same mix added around the plant to bring the surface one-half inch above the ball. Add no

17

CILPINENSE, *for early bloom in the smaller garden. The flowers may need to be protected from frost at blooming time. Try 'Cilpinense' in a tub on the patio, and you might bring it indoors for Christmas flowers.*

more than that! A retaining wall about 15 inches high should be built around raised beds to hold the medium. Another method, especially desirable where drainage is poor, is to place the plant on four-inch mounds of gravel, wash the soil from the root tips and carefully cover them with the peat-perlite mixture. In either case, the after-watering should be thorough to insure firm placement of the mixture around the roots.

GOOD DRAINAGE IMPORTANT

Generally speaking, rhododendrons can be planted in the conventional manner if drainage is good. The hole should be dug to measure four to five inches more in diameter than the ball of the plant. The bottom of the hole should be firmed to prevent settling which could result in the plant being too deep. Actually, the top of the root ball should set about an inch above the soil surface. Be sure to soak the root ball well before planting. Fill in the hole around the plant with prepared soil or with a peat-perlite mixture and barely cover the ball as you mound the soil or mix around it.

Where drainage is exceptional and rainfall is not too heavy, you might try a subsurface bed. Test the drainage first to be certain the procedure will be safe. The bed should be about 18 to 20 inches deep and perhaps 30 inches wide for a single row of rhododendrons. Follow previous recommendations for placing the root ball and covering it. Regardless of the method used, I suggest that you space most rhododendrons 3 to 4 feet apart. Of course, the distance will vary with miniature or exceptionally large types.

Choose varieties carefully, giving full consideration to the total landscape and to color combinations. By the way, never order rhododendrons by color alone; ask the dealer for information about color, growth habit and where the plant might grow well in your garden. Some rhododendrons fit into the landscape better than others, depending upon the individual situation. If space is unlimited, you can try everything from the smallest to the largest varieties. A tiny garden will accommodate only miniatures and semi-dwarf types that will not overpower the limited space.

How do I feel about using rhododendrons with other shrubs and plants? It's great, provided the over-all effect is well planned so that colors do not shout at one another and foliage textures do not clash. There are many fine evergreens and deciduous plants

Clifford A. Fenner

CHEVALIER FELIX DE SAUVAGE, *a century old hybrid still being put to good use. Frequently sold in Southern California. Highly recommended for early forcing.*

that go well together. I do think that many plants, such as rhododendrons, or rhododendrons and azaleas combined, or other plants like roses, are more effective when planted in distinct groupings. The rhododendron, an inhabitant of the most renowned gardens of the world, seems to me to be deserving of singular attention.

Rhododendrons make fine container plants for the mobile garden. The same good rules of plantings must be observed. Placement of the containers as they are moved from time to time will require careful consideration of possible adverse effects of weather and exposure that could quickly ruin a valuable plant.

Did you know that rhododendrons can be used as bonsai plants? *R. impeditum, R. radicans* and *R. serpyllifolium,* among others, serve as an excellent base for this interesting Japanese art form.

The blossoms of the rhododendron provide lovely, long-lasting, cut flowers. Always cut branches for this purpose just above a leaf whorl. Improper cutting of blooms can spoil the beauty and form of a plant. Do not leave a branch extending awkwardly in the air like an arm in a cast.

EVENING GLOW, *like a golden sunset. Mr. Van Veen was proud of this hybrid because at the time it was about the deepest yellow available in a rhododendron. Grow in slight shade for best results. In too much shade and it will not bud well. 'Evening Glow' seems to perform quite satisfactorily in the South.*

GOMER WATERER, *how beautifully the flowers crown the plant! Among the best of the hybrids for year-around attractiveness. Listed as a white, but the buds are pink and the flowers are flushed on opening. Very dependable grower in warm climates.*

This brings to mind the subject of pruning, which can be handled in the same manner described for cutting the flowers. Shaping the plant should be the primary consideration. Summer is a good time to prune rhododendrons, immediately after flowering. This will allow dormant growth buds below the cut to mature as the next growing season evolves. Pruning can be done as late as April, but the gardener must realize that he is cutting away bloom buds and will not enjoy many flowers until the next season.

In my opinion, the natural growth of rhododendrons is preferable to a formally shaped plant. I realize, though, that sometimes the plants become ragged or straggly and must be pruned. Healthy plants will stand severe cutting. By gradually removing the unwanted growth over a period of three or four years, a plant can be cut back to graft level (if a grafted plant) and new growth will start immediately. Unwanted tender growth can be removed by pinching it back to the point of origin.

Rhododendrons look their best when well-groomed. I like to see the faded florets removed promptly, rather than leaving them to dangle in space. And, when the truss has completely bloomed out, I prefer to remove it, too. The chore is simple, for the trusses snap off easily. Removing the old trusses directs energy that would be wasted on seed production into growth of lush new foliage. Another reason for taking out the dead flowers is that they harbor insects and disease which might harm the plant later.

Never cultivate rhododendrons. The mulch will keep down most of the weeds. The rhododendrons' habit of spreading growth also will discourage them. Otherwise, I'm afraid you'll have to stoop down and pull any weeds that might develop. Sorry!

Do not place rhododendrons under eaves or other places that will restrict rainfall or where falling snow or ice from roofs may result in plant breakage. The extreme brittleness of rhododendrons when they are cold makes them very susceptible to this type of damage. Protection can be arranged by having at hand some sort of overhead frame that can be put into place over endangered plants.

NATURALIZED PLANTINGS

Those of you who plan to use rhododendrons in a woodland or native setting would

(THE HONORABLE) JEAN MARIE DE MONTAGUE, *trusses of crinkled red loveliness. Probably the most popular variety in this country today. The foliage will stand strong sun but the flowers will fade too quickly. 'Jean Marie' adapts herself very well to the warm climate of the Southeast.*

do well to remember that Mother Nature, expert gardener that she is, can be given some assistance now and then. Before you plant, take a good look at the terrain, noting the plants existing there and the trees at hand. Again let me remind you of the situation involving shallow-rooted trees and rhododendrons. Especially in the case of native trees, you might consider cutting a proper-sized hole through the root system of a tree wherever you wish to place a rhododendron. Remove the clutter of old roots, place an inch or two of prepared soil in and around the sides of the hole and then line it with perforated black plastic. Place more soil on the

CUNNINGHAM'S WHITE, *white flowers are more beautiful because of yellowish blotch. The dense growth and hardiness make an excellent landscape feature. Said to be tolerant of slightly alkaline soil. There is some fall bloom in warmer areas.*

ALBERT CLOSE, *a rare blend of east and west coast native American species. The flowering season is extended by its late bloom. Heat tolerant because of R. maximum heritage.*

exposed side of the plastic and plant the rhododendron in the manner explained earlier. Not all of the tree's roots will be excluded, but the rhododendron will have a fighting chance if fed and watered extra well. There may be certain shrubs existing in the native area which offer too much competition, or whose foliage and growth patterns may not harmonize well with your rhododendrons. These native plants should be removed.

There is a basic principle which always should be considered when landscaping a home. Such plantings are meant to increase the attractiveness of your home; do not make the house a mere background for the plants. With this in mind, can you possibly suggest any plant better suited for this purpose than the rhododendron? The dwarf types are ideal subjects for foundation plantings, but the larger varieties create too great a mass of vegetation and are not in scale with the low-built modern home. Both types and those with sizes in between can be utilized in perimeter beds.

Always put yourself in the picture and visualize the appearance of the yard from the inside of your home as you gaze across the landscape, and as you stand in various parts of the yard and look in all directions between the house and the perimeter.

Looking out of the window, you do not want your view obstructed by large plants. When selecting foundation plants, give particular attention to their ultimate size and consider soft hues that will blend with the color of the house. Brighter colors and assorted sizes can be utilized in perimeter plantings. Here one could use rhododendrons and azaleas together. Earlier I said that rhododendrons deserve singular attention. But azaleas blend very well with rhododendrons in some landscape situations and certainly should not be overlooked.

Avoid geometric forms with rhododendrons. If you like doing this sort of thing, I suggest that you use something other than a rhododendron. Unnatural forms in plants become monotonous scenery and are not popular today.

MICHAEL WATERER, *named for the man who was the first to start serious rhododendron hybridizing over 150 years ago. A sturdy variety which will take quite a bit of sun.*

Leo F. Simon

BEAUTY OF FOLIAGE

Even if a rhododendron never flowered, it still would be one of the most beautiful plants you possibly could use in your landscape. This is true primarily because among the species there are so many beautiful forms, one to fit every sort of landscape situation. The intriguing manner in which some of the large-leaved varieties seem to reach out as you survey them is contrasted sharply with the smaller-leaved types that huddle their leaves closely about them, as does 'Bow Bells'. Apart from this, are the matters of leaf color and shape. Some, such as 'Sir Charles Lemon', have unique coloring beneath the leaves. You will find an extremely wide variety of shapes and sizes among the species.

GOLDSWORTH CRIMSON, *except in California not as popular as perhaps it should be. An Award of Merit plant which originally received an unjustifiably poor rating in this country. This has been corrected.*

CUTIE, snuggled in pocket of rock outcropping, it really is a cutie. A selected seedling of R. calostrotum which is quite hardy. Goes well when planted with any of the small-leaved "blues."

As you choose rhododendrons for your landscape, think of them as conversation pieces. I doubt if any plant, except perhaps the rose, elicits as much conversation as a rhododendron in full bloom. Can you think of any other large shrub that can surpass the rhododendron as an eye-opener and bring forth so many 'ohs' and 'ahs'? I can't. When you become better acquainted with the background of your own rhododendrons, you can add to the conversation by way of a bit of 'name-dropping' and over-seas history surrounding some varieties, plus a few words about the American heritage or development of others.

CARY ANN, *even the red coloring sets it apart from other reds. A low grower that is ultra floriferous. Will endure full sun conditions.*

SAPPHO, *Purplish blotches add distinction to white flowers, a powerful contrast which dominates the garden scene. Most famous of the blotched varieties. Extremely tall growing and can become quite lanky. It should be pinched and pruned back vigorously. 'Sappho' will frequently branch from the stem if cut back at a point other than a leaf whorl.*

The beauty of the foliage is further enhanced by the variety of tips, bases and margins.

There is another aspect to landscaping with rhododendrons that once was not considered. It has to do with their use in public areas and around business and industrial structures. One doesn't have to think back very many years to remember the time when a manufacturer's buildings and grounds were strictly for business. Who ever gave a thought that the morale and outlook of employees and customers might be lifted by viewing a panorama of beautiful plants in well-landscaped grounds surrounding an office or factory. No one had ever stopped to consider that the person on his way into a bank to ask for an extension of his note might receive needed inspiration from lovely floral surroundings, or that an employee might find greater pride and satisfaction in working for an organization caring enough to provide attractive landscaping. Our civilization rests upon the stewardship of the land, which unfortunately has been despoiled in many communities by intense industrialization by those who have failed to

25

The American Rhododendron Society Display Garden on Crystal Springs Island in Portland, Oregon. Towering fir trees cover the island which is reached by a foot bridge. On the left of the path 'Beauty of Littleworth' dominates the scene. 'Mrs. G. W. Leak', 'Princess Juliana' and 'Essex Scarlet' are in the background. On the other side magnificent and fragrant 'Loderi King George' in full array invariably catches the admiration of visitors.

realize their responsibility to aesthetic values. No country can despoil its land and not suffer as a result. I am gratified to see a new awakening and effort to beautify our country. I believe there is no better way to bring more lasting and arresting beauty to the landscape than with rhododendrons. I salute leaders in industry and government who have allocated the funds to landscape their properties, and I give a second salute to those who have used rhododendrons!

If you wish to receive the utmost enjoyment and lasting beauty from every dollar you spend to landscape your property, I suggest that you plan the use of your material carefully. Perspective is best on paper, rather than held in the mind. Before you plant, make a sketch or seek professional help if your landscaping needs are extensive. As a road map shows you how to go from here to there, a good plan leads you through your landscaping journey. You will arrive at the desired destination even though you may stop from time to time to catch your breath and recoup your finances. It is far easier and more economical, in the final accounting, to landscape from a blueprint than to stumble along by trial and error. Your property will be more beautiful and valuable and you will receive more enjoyment from it.

CHAPTER THREE

The Temperature Factor

 In this chapter I wish to convey two principal ideas. First, I want to stress the proper consideration of climatic factors affecting the use of rhododendrons in the garden, with particular emphasis on the fact that you can grow rhodies successfully wherever you live. If you are fortunate enough to live in a climate comparable to the Pacific Northwest, you can grow almost any of the varieties. In some other areas you will be limited to the use of certain rhododendrons, or it will be necessary to amend the climatic situation in various ways so that a wider range of varieties can be grown.

Secondly, I think it is important to place special emphasis on what rhododendrons can achieve for you in the landscape. At the close of this chapter I relay some thoughts which may not have occurred to you concerning home landscaping that creates climatic effects beneficial to you in return for the attention you have given to the plants.

THE CLIMATE

There is still much mystery about the climatic factors of plant life. Scientists and those of us concerned with plant production are learning constantly, sometimes by design, sometimes by accident. I want to help you avoid some pitfalls that might discourage you from using rhododendrons. Perhaps you have had an unfortunate experience with them in the past, or you have heard that "so-and-so", a good gardener, did not have any luck with his rhododendrons. It is a pretty safe bet that any such problem resulted from unwise selection of varieties, poor soil conditions, improper placement or lack of protection. Extra attention to choosing varieties, altering the soil and providing the necessary protection means the difference between failure and success. From my personal experiences, I believe sincerely that RHODODENDRONS are for you!

When it comes right down to choosing those particular varieties for your garden, Chapter XI deserves careful study. It includes those which I consider to be among the very best rhododendrons. You will notice the hardiness indications, as well as color, growth habit, and other information which will make selecting varieties easier.

With rhododendrons, as with most other plants used in the landscape, both minimum and maximum temperatures must be considered. Other factors are wind, frost effect on early growth, shade, and light intensity. Then we determine the means of protecting the plants from the various climatic problems by use of proper positioning, adequate moisture, mulching and wind breaks. Let's start with the subject of high temperature.

WHERE TEMPERATURES ARE HIGH

High temperature and low humidity go hand in hand to cause problems for many rhododendrons. It is true that rhododendrons are found growing naturally where temperatures may reach high degrees, but usually these plants are found at relatively high altitudes and are blessed with considerable humidity. I think the greatest heat problem is caused by rapid alternation between cool and hot summer temperatures. A rhododendron finds it difficult to adjust to sudden changes and you must be prepared to give it some assistance.

Tied in closely with the hot-dry problem is the matter of light intensity. This is not the same in all parts of the country. Generally, rhododendrons grow naturally where the light intensity is modified by long rainy seasons (this is true of the Pacific Northwest) or by frequent high fog. Here in Ore-

R. LUTESCENS, *an exciting species. In spring the new foliage comes out in a glossy bronze-red and then slowly turns to green throughout the summer. An excellent companion plant for 'Praecox'.*

FASTUOSUM PLENUM *(Fastuosum Flore Pleno), fascinating double effect makes it a favorite lavender. The flowers are long-lasting and are most attractive floated in a shallow bowl. You can use this hybrid between varieties to avoid a color clash.*

gon, I have noted a difference in the appearance of rhododendrons during a normal summer compared to an infrequent hot, dry summer. This is simply because the combination of high light intensity and low humidity produce unfavorable conditions. There really is no variety of rhododendron that can be described as a sun lover.

The disadvantages of high light intensity, high temperature and low humidity can be offset. Shade is the key word. We learned as youngsters that shade certainly reduces the temperature. The difference may be as much as 15 to 50 degrees between full sun and a shaded area. This can make a decided difference to rhododendrons.

Let me caution you, though, about the amount of shade. Dense shade is not ideal for rhododendrons. The plants grow lushly

NOYO CHIEF, *have you ever seen more wonderful foliage? And flowers to match, too. Those leaves also have a plastered fawn tomentum beneath. Has been sold as the species, R. zeylanicum, and also as the older name, R. kingianum.*

but do not flower well. They like broken shade, such as the intermittent light provided by shade trees or lath structures. The north side of a building, protected from a hot mid-day sun but receiving the slanted morning and evening rays and reflected light, is a favorite site for rhododendrons. (Remember the warning about shallow-rooted trees in Chapter II, for they can rob your plants of needed moisture, calling for extra irrigation.)

SHADE STRUCTURES

Designs for some very attractive shade structures are available today. The traditional house of wood lath or metal, or a house built of wooden material wider than lath, still is utilized. I have been impressed by Saran or plastic cloth used for shade structures. It can be purchased in various densities, providing just the right amount of shade, and comes in a pleasant green color that harmonizes with the landscape. Then, of course, there is the natural method of providing shade over your patio or other garden area by using suitable vines. So that you do not blot out all the sunlight, choose a vine with a loose open growth habit. An existing vine with dense foliage should be pruned to afford the proper amount of shade.

The use of surface or overhead irrigation and/or misting will help in controlling the temperature during the heat of the summer. Use overhead sprinklers rather than surface irrigation if at all possible. The temperature of the air will be reduced as well as that of the soil and root area. Tie this in with proper mulching, and you have the means of lowering plant temperatures considerably. (See Chapter VI for more information on mulching procedures and irrigation practices recommended for rhododendrons.)

I have found that "burning" or browning of leaves from lack of moisture on hot days can be prevented by continuous mist-type overhead irrigation. Do not over-do it, though, and water-log the soil. Done judiciously, I guarantee that rhodies will admirably survive some difficult periods of high temperature. Perhaps you have heard that it is hazardous to apply overhead moisture on a bright, sunny day because the water droplets magnify the sun's rays. This is somewhat of an old wives' tale and is certainly not true of rhododendrons and other plants with waxy leaf surfaces which do not hold water. I assure you that commercial rhododendron growers apply water when it is needed. We would not allow our plants to suffer through a hot day, nor would we wait until evening to irrigate them.

I believe that gardeners living in areas of hot summer temperatures and low humidity would profit greatly from the use of misting nozzles. Such nozzles should be operated during lengthy periods of hot, dry

COUNTESS OF DERBY, *also listed as 'Eureka Maid'. A 'Pink Pearl' type with foliage, truss and flower slightly larger, and the color a little pinker. Also similar to 'Professor Hugo de Vries' which blooms about a week later.*

BLUE TIT and YELLOW HAMMER, contrasting beauties will arrest attention in any garden. Also goes well with the daffodils. Most blue and purple rhododendrons are late while the yellows generally have an early blooming period. Will grow well in full sun, but the flowers will not fade so fast if there is a little shade. 'Blue Tit' is quite effective in mass plantings. 'Yellow Hammer' may flower in the fall but it will still have adequate color in the spring. Cut it back after spring flowering to control the shape.

weather. They provide the desired effects of cooling the air and raising the humidity without the danger of applying too much water to the root area. Check with a reliable dealer before purchasing misting equipment and obtain his expert advice about the proper size nozzle. A nozzle used in a lath house, where the rate of evaporation is less, would differ from one for the out-of-doors.

WIND AND WINTER

Before discussing winter temperature, I will say a few words about wind and its effect on rhododendrons. Wind must be considered in relation to the cold of winter as well as summer's heat. Normally we link low

BOULE DE NEIGE, *the French meaning is "ball of snow". A hardy, top-quality grower for the low landscape requirement. Performs well in the sun, but shade is best where lace wing fly is a problem.*

humidity with summer. But, low humidity can occur during winter as well. Besides the breakage that winter obviously may cause to rhododendrons and other plants, there is the problem of dehydration. All plants lose moisture at a highly increased rate when dry winds buffet them for a lengthy period of time. The gardener in an area of prevailing winds during summer or winter should provide windbreaks to protect his rhododendrons. Other plants or trees, lath barriers, or fencing serve this purpose. The large-leaved varieties need more protection than the small-leaved plants, both from the standpoint of dehydration and breakage. I particularly like to use a fence that allows air movement but breaks the main force of the wind. A board-on-board, picket or lath-wire fence is ideal. Select plants for windbreaks that

do not become a problem by growing too large or too dense.

No one can supply all the answers to the questions of hardiness and winter's effects on rhododendrons, but I can give you some practical guidelines. Hardy rhododendrons, like other plants normally capable of withstanding low temperatures, can be hard hit when winter strikes suddenly. We experienced this in Oregon in November, 1955,

DAVID, *new growth frames rich-red truss. A newer hybrid which seems to be replacing some of the older "reds", particularly 'Earl of Athlone', which it resembles exactly in flower. However, the plant habit is much better.*

SCINTILLATION, *the best known of the seedlings from the C. O. Dexter collection. The parentage has been lost, but quite possibly it is a R. fortunei hybrid. A rugged plant which will take much punishment, but it does best with some shade in extreme sun conditions.*

means made necessary by unusual circumstances. If there is a rhododendron variety you "just can't resist" but its hardiness is marginal for your climate, provide it with extra protection from the start. You might cover the plant with a burlap or plastic covered frame. Do not allow plastic to touch the plant or freezing will result. Remove the plastic immediately when sunlight is bright so that the plant will not suffer from heat and lack of air. Another method is that of the old-fashioned gardener who encircles each plant with wire-fencing and fills the space between plant and fencing with evergreen boughs. These serve as effective wind barriers, too.

It takes a while for the inner temperature of a plant to drop. An hour or two of atmospheric temperature lower than that indicated by the plant's hardiness rating is not apt to damage a rhododendron. I do not

DR. A. BLOK, *like a beautiful painting. A 'Pink Pearl' type with larger foliage and flowers, and the suggestion of yellow in the throat. The huge flower buds are particularly intriguing. Frequently this variety is sold as 'Dr. O. Blok'.*

when summer-like temperatures dropped overnight to winter levels. Naturally, some rhododendrons were hurt. However, the rhodies performed magnificently compared to many other plants. A great many rhododendrons took the "big freeze" without injury, and almost all damaged plants made a fast comeback the following spring. To avoid unnecessary problems, check the hardiness ratings listed in Chapter XI. Provide normal protection by proper placement, mulching, and windbreaks, and by any other

MADAME MASSON, *golden splotches like money in the bank. A larger growing white which does well in sun or shade.*

the year when so many plants are without foliage. I suggest that mulch protection be provided as a general rule. Wait until an unusual cold spell is forecast and then apply further protection as needed.

Varieties you know to be incapable of withstanding cold winters should be grown in containers. These, along with choice garden specimens that you feel are threatened by severe winter weather, should be moved into a cool greenhouse or other protected enclosure. Be certain there is adequate light available, because they will not take kindly to darkness. If a plant is not too large, it can be moved quite easily. A rhododendron accepts transplanting very well, especially if a large soil ball is taken with it. In early spring, it should go back outdoors. You need

MADAME FR. J. CHAUVIN, *an Award of Merit hybrid. There are not too many good hardy pink varieties. Also a good performer in the warmer South.*

think you will receive full enjoyment from your rhodies if you regularly cover them each winter. Half the pleasure of owning these lovely plants is viewing their evergreen symmetry from the window at the time of

MRS. CHARLES E. PEARSON, *elegant foliage providing year around attractiveness. Should be used more. Quite possibly a little more hardy than rated, and she has proven herself in warm climates. A good screen plant.*

not always think in terms of a frost-free greenhouse for protection for moved-in rhododendrons. If the root ball is protected from severe freezing and the foliage is protected from wind and bright sun, rapid fluctuations of temperature that cause moisture loss will be minimized.

ABOUT FROST

In some areas frost is a problem in the spring for the early blooming rhododendrons. In Oregon some varieties normally start new growth early in the spring and, occasionally, even in late winter. As a general rule, spring frost damage is light and not serious enough to cause concern. However, I advise you to place the "early-riser" rhododendrons in a well protected spot in the landscape. Almost every garden has an area with fewer exposure hazards. Frost occurs first where the cold air settles in the lowest part of a garden. Very little elevation is required to achieve a life-saving difference in temperature. A variety may be frost damaged at the lowest point, but remain untouched if placed only a few feet higher. Set your less hardy rhododendrons at the higher points where there is gentle air movement. Of course, there is no substitute for adequate physical protection from cold, windy weather.

COOLING THE AIR

There are benefits to be derived from rhododendrons and other plants, in addition to their beauty of flower, foliage and form. If you believe that man invented air conditioning, you are due for a jolt. Nature has had an air conditioning system since the beginning of time. Man-made air conditioning, a modern luxury that provides a comfortable indoor environment, was first enjoyed in the Garden of Eden, as a cool breeze filtered through the trees. Nature's cycle of depositing moisture in the form of rain and reclaiming it into the atmosphere by means of evaporation and transpiration from the leaves of plants produces a cooling effect. Because of their lush foliage and the moisture they release, I believe that rhododendrons are among the best garden air conditioners.

Where do people go to find relief from the city's heat? They seek the ocean with its salt water and sea breezes; they camp near a secluded lake where trees and water combine for soothing solace; or they fish the mountain stream and breathe the air sweet with the scent of pine. Regardless of where one goes in search of cooling comfort, the principal ingredients of water, moving air and plant life are always present. The first air conditioning "machine" belongs to nature, and man only discovered the concept and brought it indoors. I maintain that a

ICE CUBE, *a splendid new hybrid just introduced by Mr. Shammarello. An outstanding white variety for cold regions which blooms a little later than 'Belle Heller' and is a bit tighter in growth habit.*

ALICE, *a crown jewel befitting a queen's garden. The heavy foliage will stand strong sunlight. Allow plenty of room since this variety will not branch well if it is pruned back too far.*

ILAM VIOLET, *see how perfectly this violet beauty improves the landscape. A free flowering hybrid with aromatic foliage. Originated in New Zealand.*

well-planned garden with trees and large-leaved plants like rhododendrons provide the finest possible exterior air-conditioning and, in turn, cools the air within the house.

Many homes west of the Cascade Mountains do not need mechanized air conditioning because of the abundant trees and shrubs nearby. The vegetation is a "cooling pad" through which nature draws its air currents thereby supplying relief from the heat of the sun. Rhododendrons placed so that prevailing breezes must filter through their foliage, tall trees to divert the mid-day and afternoon sun, and vines on a trellis all will aid in reducing the temperature in a home at least ten degrees. Just think, beautiful landscaping with a bonus of air conditioning!

CHAPTER FOUR

What To Look For
When Buying Rhododendrons

How hardy? Which color? What is the growth habit? How will I know if I will get what I want? These and other questions are associated with the purchase of rhododendrons. A "blind" date made on hearsay or the recommendation of a friend can be disappointing. Similarly, a rhododendron purchased without forethought and investigation could prove to be a disappointment.

Rhododendrons are long-lasting, quality plants for the landscape, if properly selected. First, be cautious about buying the "bargain basement" type from supermarket sales lots, or other places where the plants may have suffered from neglect. These plants may also be a "pig-in-a-poke" purchase simply because there is no assurance that they are true to the name and color represented on the tag. There probably is no malicious or fraudulent intent, but unfortunately considerable confusion exists concerning names of rhododendron varieties. I explain this later in the chapter. Be certain you know which variety you want. Then, by patronizing a reputable dealer with a thorough knowledge of rhododendrons, you will take home the plant for which you asked.

ABOUT NAMES
In assembling my notes for this chapter, it occurred to me that the expression "duke's

mixture" might have originated as the result of the manner in which some rhododendron growers handled nomenclature many years ago. Let me explain. A varietal name should be given to one particular seedling of a group of hybrid progeny resulting from a single cross. This new plant is called a "clone." Its identity usually can be maintained only if it is propagated by asexual means, such as cuttings, layers, grafting or budding. This new variety will carry exactly the same foliage, bloom and growth habit as the original seedling, except on a rare occasion when a mutation occurs.

The early rhododendron breeders followed a procedure of assigning one name to all seedlings resulting from crossing the same parent varieties. But, all such seedlings are not equal. Some may grow less vigorously than others. Often there are variations in bloom color, form, and the growth habit. The problem was compounded over the years as crosses were made between known and unknown varieties. When the nursery trade started offering these named groups, it was not unusual to see two plants, one with a red bloom and the other with a white flower, bearing the same name. This confusion still persists to a minor degree.

You may be wondering why I am giving this rather technical information. My purpose is to advise you how to get "true-to-name" rhodies. It is very important to buy

QUEEN MARY AND GOLDSWORTH YELLOW, *a mass planting which demonstrates the versatility of rhododendrons in the landscape. The dark leathery foliage of 'Queen Mary' offers a year around handsome appearance.*

plants grown only by nurserymen using the code of nomenclature established a number of years ago by the American Rhododendron Society and the Royal Horticulture Society of England. The difficult, necessary work on nomenclature and registry is carried on by experts in the rhododendron world. They have established these basic rules: Seedling group names cannot be used; individual new plants introduced to the market must carry a name exclusive to that plant; and unnamed seedlings must be sold as such or must be identified by parentage. In the past, the American Rhododendron Society has listed both clonal and group names, designating the latter with a "G." Now, only clones are registered by both societies. Some years have passed since the organizations started following this procedure, and many new varieties have been developed which carry the correct clonal name. If you buy one of these varieties, you can be quite certain that it is true to name. There still are some plants sold which are propagated from those kinds developed during the group-name era. This is not entirely wrong since many of these plants have merit.

Undoubtedly, you now understand the two major pitfalls to avoid when purchasing rhododendrons: ordering plants by color only from an unknown dealer, and buying by a variety name which is a group identification rather than clonal.

May I suggest that you use my list of recommended varieties in Chapter XI. I have spent many hours selecting these varieties and checking their descriptions, hardiness ratings, and other important characteristics which will help you in choosing the best kinds for your garden. If you purchase them from a reputable dealer, you will get plants that fit the descriptions.

MADAME DE BRUIN, *the largest tight trusses of almost cherry red against the light green, wavy foliage is a beautiful contrast. Flower and foliage require shade. Does not do well in the Mid-Atlantic coastal area.*

KNOW WHAT YOU SEEK

Perhaps you feel the name of a rhododendron is less important than the color and height. To start, then, visit a reliable garden center or nursery when the rhododendrons are in bloom and select the varieties that suit your taste and needs. The variety names may seem inconsequential at the moment, but I bet that their significance will increase as you become more familiar with rhodies. Keep a list of varieties and attach a permanent name tag to each of your plants. In time, their names will become as familiar to you as the names of your friends.

You will not only be better informed and more confident about your selections, but you will enjoy your rhododendrons more if you take time to read about their requirements and fascinating history. You will thus

WINDBEAM, every bit as fascinating as its name indicates. Those neat little leaves are aromatic. Easy to grow in most any location, and it will survive at 25 below zero.

PURPLE SPLENDOUR, the dark purple appearance is made more intense by the black center of the flower. Try planting with yellows such as 'Goldfort' or 'Evening Glow'. Will grow in sun or shade.

avoid those questionable merchants who peddle rhododendrons door to door. Plants offered from the street usually are candidates for the dump heap. They are mostly collected native plants or nursery discards with a minimal chance of survival. Only a horticulture expert would know if they are in good condition. Often they have been out of the ground for a long period and are dried out, even though the root ball is wrapped in burlap. If the plants are large, they probably did not receive the expert digging required for their size. These "bargains" are transported to the peddling area with more thought of profit than customer satisfaction.

Well grown, named varieties cost more than collected plants or unnamed seedlings, but they are more than worth the difference. Perhaps the neophyte will be less tempted to try these inferior plants when he realizes that a rhododendron breeder may throw away hundreds, even thousands, of seedlings before he finds one he considers worthy of keeping and naming.

There are many characteristics which a plant breeder considers in his search for new rhododendrons: hardiness and disease resistance, flower color, size of bloom, truss shape, plant size and form, foliage and all around good looks. Another factor is ease of propagation. Some varieties root and develop much better than others. Those kinds that are difficult to propagate seldom are grown commercially in large quantities. They cost too much to produce and hence are too expensive for most home gardeners.

CARMEN, wonderful dwarf with handsome foliage and red bells which look you in the eye. The dark ruby bells are brilliant when the plant is located so the blooms catch the sunlight. Requires more than normal good drainage.

JAN DEKENS, wouldn't you enjoy this high-crowned, glossy-foliaged loveliness in your landscape? A good screen plant which will take the sun.

LADY BLIGH, *a tremendous plant, here framed with background of trees. The many shades of color from strawberry red to light pink is a fascinating picture.*

EXAMINE PLANTS

If you live in a hot climate, look for a graft mark on a rhododendron before buying. If the trunk shows that the plant has been grafted, it is not suitable for you. This does not hold true for cooler climates. A graft somewhat restricts circulation of sap and a grafted rhododendron often has a difficult time during hot weather. Experiments in the Houston, Texas area have shown that plants grafted on *R. ponticum* root stock are quite susceptible to root rot because of poor circulation. This problem is becoming of less concern, however, since most growers have eliminated grafting as a method of commercial propagation.

In Chapter II, I talked a bit about balled and container-grown plants. Actually, rhododendrons are moved quite easily. It is important that you buy plants with an adequate root ball which has been kept moist. The root ball of a rhododendron on display should be "heeled" (buried) in damp sawdust or soil. Most of the varieties suitable for your area should be available at a first class nursery or garden center. If you have become a rhodie "fancier," or are approaching this elite category, you probably will have to turn to a rhododendron specialist to obtain rare varieties.

Do not hesitate to examine a dealer's stock at close range. If you have previously learned the characteristics of certain rhododendrons, you will know exactly how their foliage should look. It may range from a pale to a dark green, depending upon variety. If a normally deep green foliaged rhododendron appears on the sales lot wearing a paler shade, it would be well to look elsewhere for that variety. I think that most conscientious gardeners are able to discern when foliage is fresh and vibrant. The stance of rhododendron foliage varies. The leaves of some varieties tend to droop a little; others stand straight out from the stem. Be sure to examine a plant carefully for damaged foliage, branches and buds.

Rhododendrons fit every kind of landscape. Witness this use beneath a balcony in the Spanish type atmosphere of California. The Dutch breeders produced about a dozen hybrids widely used today which are variations of 'Pink Pearl'. Most of them are quite distinct in habit and flower. All of these 'Pink Pearl' types thrive beautifully in the warm climate of Southern California.

TEMPERATURE TALK

I have already said quite a bit about temperature and the hardiness of individual rhododendrons. You will find the hardiness rating and other information for each variety listed in Chapter XI. That, however, is not the full picture of rhododendron hardiness. The -15 degree rating of 'Gomer Waterer' or the similar hardiness of 'Pink Twins' is exactly right under "normal" conditions. All the rhododendron experts in the world probably could not define the diverse reactions

Charles Kassler

CAROLINE, *pointed buds open into fragrant flowers. An exceptionally large, strong root system which helps it to survive where other rhodies might fail. Flowers are heavy-textured. Foliage will discolor when exposed to strong sun conditions.*

of one particular variety, exposed to the same low temperature, but in separated locations and grown under different cultural conditions. The low temperatures in your own landscape often vary from one area to another, and should have a bearing on the placement of varieties. The temperature in your garden may differ considerably from a neighbor's garden, one down the street or across town, because of terrain, elevation,

wind and other factors. Do not be fooled when you refer to a hardiness map for guidance and observe that the minimum temperature for your area is -5 degrees or -15 degrees. Remember that this is a general rating, not a specific one for your particular garden. If you wish, conduct a series of winter temperature tests in your garden, keeping in mind the circumstantial factors I have discussed.

WHITE PEARL, *a vigorous plant which will grow as wide as its height. Once known as Guantlettii, and more recently as Halopeanum. A successful performer in Texas.*

The actual hardiness of rhododendrons, and other plants too, is influenced by how, as well as where, the plant is grown. It is true that heredity and particular characteristics determine innate hardiness. But the amount of nitrogen and water a plant has received during its growth period also is an important factor. Hold the amount of phosphorus and potassium in the soil at a desirable level. Phosphorus contributes to the general hardiness of all plants. Potassium is believed to increase a plant's ability to resist disease, cold and other adverse conditions.

A soft, continuing-to-grow plant is more susceptible to cold, particularly if it is planted in the fall. Spring planting allows time for a rhododendron to become established before winter, especially if a late summer has not extended the growing season. The movement of northern-grown plants to southern sales areas, and vice-versa, has a tendency to confuse growth periods and further complicate the reliability of hardiness ratings. However, I have found that dependable nurserymen obtain rhododendrons early enough for the plants to adjust to local conditions before the time of sale. Growers plan their production schedules so that plants are in prime condition at shipping time. The ultimate owners of these rhododendrons will experience a minimum of trouble from winter's cold, and from other hazards as well. All that these plants need is your continued "tender loving care."

CHAPTER FIVE

Making Your Soil Right For Rhododendrons

If you find yourself growing taller with each step you take through your planned garden area because of the mud that sticks to your shoes, you have a problem! You can be certain that the soil is too heavy for any type of plant. After a period of dry weather, it will become as hard as concrete. This soil is especially unsuited to rhododendrons and azaleas.

This chapter is about soils in general, what can be done to amend them and how to insure good drainage. I also give you specific information about the best kinds of soil for rhododendrons. I think it is important to see the whole picture, so that you will understand how to derive maximum benefits from your particular soil.

At one time, I was "blessed" with the type of soil mentioned in the first paragraph. I refer to it as "contractor's" or "builder's" soil. In reality, it is the subsoil which has been scooped out of a basement excavation or uncovered in grading a lot for a new house. The topsoil, the result of na-

ture's work during thousands of years, is buried and lost. It is a wise contractor who first pushes back the layer of topsoil before excavating and grading, and who after building the house, spreads the subsoil and covers it with stock-piled topsoil. The lucky new owner of this property can grow a green carpet of grass, shade trees and prize-winning rhododendrons.

What can be done with subsoil? At considerable expense, it can be removed and replaced with topsoil from another site. If this is not possible, you work, and work some more, to build a new organic soil. There is no magic formula for quick and easy success. For each soil improvement you make, you will be rewarded by a gratifying improvement in the performance of your rhododendrons and other plants.

SOIL TEXTURE

I feel very strongly about the importance of soil texture. Details of soil structure, fertility and the "mystery" of pH (acidity-alkalinity) will be covered later. Without the proper texture, your efforts to provide the many other requirements of a prime soil will be wasted. Soils with poor texture, mostly caused by too little organic matter, will not support the bacteria which are essential for normal plant growth.

It would be wonderful if you could recondition every square foot of soil in your new garden before planting. However, the top

VERNUS, opening with the daffodils and dogwoods, spring arrives also with this new hybrid. A most welcome extension of the blooming season for colder climates.

David G. Leach

47

12 inches of soil on a 50 x 100 foot lot weigh a million pounds, give or take a few pounds, so not many gardeners find enough "oomph" to recondition the whole lot the first year.

Instead of trying to handle all the soil, concentrate on the portion needing improvement the most. If this happens to be a planned rhododendron bed, give that area your attention. Rhodies are valuable plants, and they will give you beauty and pleasure for many years. Upkeep will be at a minimum if the soil is right from the beginning. Some weeding, a small amount of fertilizer, additional mulch, and moisture is all that the

shallow-rooted rhododendrons need. What a welcome relief from the back-breaking chore of spading a great mass of soil!

Can you judge the texture of a soil by its color? Absolutely not! It can be black, brown or red and still not promote good root development and top growth. If the general physical make-up of the soil is poor, the mere addition of fertilizer will not correct the situation.

As a simple test of your soil's texture, take a handful of moist soil and squeeze it tightly. If it compacts into a hard ball, it is too heavy and more humus and sand are

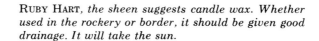

RUBY HART, *the sheen suggests candle wax. Whether used in the rockery or border, it should be given good drainage. It will take the sun.*

needed. It is too light if it crumbles when you open your hand. If the soil holds together after pressure is released, but shatters when dropped gently, the texture is good. It has good aeration and drainage qualities, and will retain the proper amount of moisture.

A heavy soil will stick to your shoes, will build up on your hoe and is difficult to spade. Water will stand in puddles on its surface. A light sandy soil is easy to spade and water drains through it too well. The additional water it requires not only leaches fertilizer from the soil but makes sprinkling a chore.

To convert a too-heavy soil to one with the friable texture needed for vigorous growth, add sand to help provide aeration and drainage, and organic matter in the form of compost, peat moss, and leaf mold. While Eastern sawdust is considered undesirable, it is generally used in the West. It

Sylvan by nature, most rhododendrons are well suited for the woodsy environment and blend in nicely with the native trees and companion shrubs. 'Susan' is in the right foreground, 'Unique' and 'Blue Diamond' near the front entrance.

MRS. G. W. LEAK, *excites interest whenever seen. Sometimes sold in California as 'Cottage Gardens Pride'. Grows equally well in sun or shade. It is a good cutflower.*

should be aged for best results. Fresh sawdust causes the bacteria in the soil to "reach" for more nitrogen, and sometimes extra phosphorous, for help in the process of decomposition. Unless you replenish the supply, plants will suffer from a lack of nutrients. A starting rule-of-thumb to correct this imbalance is 12 pounds of ammonium sulphate per 1000 square feet of surface for each inch of sawdust worked into the soil. Please note, I said "worked into" the soil. Sawdust used strictly for mulching has a different effect. This formula does not apply to the general feeding of plants which is explained later.

When a soil is too light and sandy, add the types of humus mentioned above. This

when the soil is not too wet. Walking on or working wet soil will damage its structure; so let it dry a bit before turning the cover crop under. Break up the large clumps of earth as you spade, and save yourself the extra work of crushing rock-hard clods later. Rotary tilling is easier than and superior to spading. Tillers can be rented from many garden centers and stores specializing in garden equipment rentals.

SOIL STRUCTURE

Soil structure is different from soil texture. Many gardeners confuse them. The

BUTTERFLY, *red flecking like paprika on something good to eat. Grow in the background because the small leaves give the appearance of too much openness. Quite heat tolerant, and likes sun or shade.*

SCARLET WONDER, *what a landscape picture! A new Dietrich Hobbie hybrid which inevitably will become very popular. The flowers have good substance, the foliage sheen remains the year around, cold hardy, heat tolerant, and a shrublet with character.*

will improve its moisture-holding ability and prevent excessive drainage and leaching, all of which are factors vitally important to rhododendrons.

If you wish to make this job of rejuvenating your soil as economical as possible, use cover crops and all available compost. Remove the oldest, most decomposed materials from the bottom of the compost pile, screen it and work it into the soil.

Cover crops (green manure) are a wonderful organic material for soil building, although they are not as long-lasting as some forms of humus. A cover crop should be turned under in the spring or early summer,

CHIONOIDES, *among the best of the late flowering white compacts. An early English variety in which the name was an attempt to make a hybrid sound like a rare species. Looks good with 'Purple Splendour'.*

structure refers to the manner in which soil particles (sand, silt or clay) are bound together as granules. Texture is a more or less permanent property of soil, depending of course on husbandry. It refers only to the proportionate amount of sand, silt or clay particles present in the soil. In spite of puddling, baking and other forces, soil texture remains essentially the same, but the arrangement of the particles, the soil structure, will be changed. When particles of a clay or a clay-loam soil function independently of one another, plants cannot use those soils succcessfully. Particles must be grouped together in stable granules that will not be broken down by water.

Repeated wetting and drying of soils result in formation of stable granules. Humus, finely divided organic matter, acts as a cementing material throughout the mass of soil, contracting and pressing the particles together. It will hold the particles together when completely dry. It is obvious then, that humus is essential to proper soil structure. Grasses add much organic material to the soil and build an almost ideal structure.

Basically, there are three types of soils structures: grain, crumb and puddled. The grainy soil is loose and open with large individual pore spaces which allow ample air circulation and water movement. Cultivation is easy and the soil warms quickly. A commercial grower wanting an early crop will use sandy, warm soil because it stimulates

SIR CHARLES LEMON, *dark anthers on a field of white. Note the upper golden "freckles". Worth growing for the foliage alone. The orange indumentum contrasts well with the countless white flowers of fragrance.*

RAMAPO, *interesting landscape material for the rock garden or low border. Plantings in large drifts are rewarding. Extreme hardiness and a preference for sun and exposure. The foliage takes on a deep metallic color in the winter. A Guy Nearing introduction.*

growth and can be cultivated soon after a rainfall or irrigation. There is a major fault to sandy loose soil, however, especially from the standpoint of rhododendrons. It is incapable of holding sufficient moisture and nutrients, and is apt to be infertile and constantly dry. This problem soil will be helped greatly by the addition of humus.

The crumb-type structure, which usually occurs in a loam soil, is ideal for most plants, including rhododendrons. It contains some particles that are large and function separately; other particles are medium to small in size and cluster together to form granules and aggregates. There are some large pore spaces (as in sandy soil) that facilitate drainage and air movement, and numberless

UNKNOWN WARRIOR, *popular as an early-blooming red. The plant habit is hard to control when young. However, it does improve with age. Slight shade is best for the flower color.*

LADY CLEMENTINE MITFORD, *pink ball and handsome shiny foliage would make any garden visitor detour for a closer look. There is a white tomentum on the new growth. Will take full sun and the hot climate of the South.*

small pore spaces (as in a clay soil) which retain water and nutrients. In other words, a crumb structure contains features of the other two types.

Puddled soil structure is the clay type with a majority of extremely fine particles. It should be amended by the addition of sand and humus. Correctly managed, granules and aggregates of the proper sizes will develop from the fine particles. A loose, friable soil that retains moisture and fertility will result. On the other hand, the aggregates of a loam soil can be broken down by mishandling and can produce a puddled soil.

Early spring beauty arrives before the leaves on the trees when rhodies are present in the landscape. 'Cream Crest' is accented by the various early "pinks."

When the soil structure is in top condition, your rhodies will receive generous amounts of moisture and nutrients, and will respond with healthy growth and masses of blooms.

ABOUT DRAINAGE

It would take an entire book to explain every detail of soil drainage. I will cover the highlights, discuss some of the major problems and attempt to supply the solutions.

Earlier in this chapter, I mention "contractor's" soil and its relationship to soil structure. Construction of a new home can effect changes in the soil other than reversing the topsoil and subsoil layers. The weight of bulldozers and other heavy equipment, piles of lumber and materials, and the heavy step of many workmen, often on ground soaked by rain, compact and alter the soil structure until drainage is practically nil. You are certain to be disappointed if you set out rhododendrons and other plants in such poor soil. In addition to improving the upper layer of soil, sub-soiling is needed, and possibly some more drastic aid to drainage. Sub-soiling will help to break up the

R. WILLIAMSIANUM, cascading leaves form a mound of green tumbling over rocks. The parent of many fine hybrids, and passing on to its progeny wonderful plant habit as well as heat, wind and sun tolerance. This species produces hanging, rosy-pink flowers, and it seems to bloom equally well in sun, part sun, or shade.

compacted subsoil and permit excess water to drain away.

Even when there has been no compaction of topsoil, but a sub-surface hard pan exists, sub-soiling may be necessary to prevent collection of water on top of the hard pan. The roots of plants will be wet constantly and will not receive enough air for normal growth.

The problem may be so acute that sub-soiling alone will not solve it, but other means are available. Make all necessary corrections before planting to avoid a life-long battle. If drainage is very bad and the topsoil has been lost, or badly mixed with subsoil in the shuffle of bulldozer and workmen, it would be advisable to construct covered ditches or lay drain tile before bringing in new topsoil.

Still another problem is the property plagued with a layer of rock not far from the surface. I know of one area just south of Portland, Oregon, where a thin layer of soil covers an almost solid sheet of rock. A property owner must resort to hauling in earth and building up his whole garden. The only other alternative is to plant only shallow-rooted material such as annuals, some perennials and a few shrubs. Even these do not perform well in many cases.

There are areas throughout the country where a great deal of rain falls each year. Combined with the runoff from a heavy annual snowfall, like in the Cascade Mountains near my home, this produces a high water table. Other conditions, such as a sub-surface spring or a natural catch basin for water draining from surrounding higher

CATAWBIENSE ALBUM, a selected white hybrid from the native species which grows in the Carolinas. Hardy to 25 below zero, this variety will perform well under the most adverse growing conditions.

MARYKE, *petals which will arouse any gardener's interest. My father liked this the best of his hybrids and pronounced it, Ma-rye-ka, with the accent on the second syllable. A prolific bloomer which takes the sun quite well.*

areas, cause a water level close to the surface. They all add up to excessive moisture and a need for special drainage facilities.

The best drainage results are achieved by the use of tile. Perforated plastic tile is available now and apparently is as effective as the standard clay and concrete types. Place the tile at least two feet and not more than three feet below the soil surface. As you dig the trench for the tile, separate the topsoil from the subsoil so that each can be returned to its proper place after laying the tile.

An area about 25 x 25 feet or less will need only one line of tile. If the area is larger, space ditches about 20 feet apart and use four inch pipe, draining them into a larger line, if necessary. The starting tile should have its upper end nestled in a pocket of gravel or stones. Plan the system so that there will be a fall of at least three inches for each 100 feet. Tiles must be tightly butted together and laid flat in the trench with no air pockets beneath or around them. If no city ordinance prevents it, drain the tile into a storm sewer. Otherwise, lay the tile to drain into a large, properly constructed dry well.

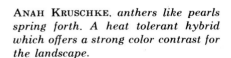

ANAH KRUSCHKE. *anthers like pearls spring forth. A heat tolerant hybrid which offers a strong color contrast for the landscape.*

C.I.S., *as thrilling a color contrast as one can imagine. Named in honor of the late Claude I. Sersanous, Past President of the American Rhododendron Society and leader in the development of the National Rhododendron Test Gardens at Portland. Individual florets are four inches across and are produced in abundance. Does best with afternoon shade.*

Sub-surface drainage can also be accomplished by digging sloping ditches to a depth of about two feet, half filling them with coarse cinders, crushed rock or gravel. Cover the stones with a layer of strawgrass or similar material to prevent soil from washing into the lower part. Then fill the remainder of the ditch with topsoil.

There is yet another simple way to correct minor drainage problems in the garden. It consists merely of raising the level of flower beds about six inches above the level of the lawn. This will amply handle an inch or two of flood water from a sudden rain or over-watering of the lawn. I do not recommend this system to solve a chronic problem that is preventing your use of rhododendrons or other choice shrubs.

IMPORTANCE OF HUMUS

Rhodies will develop healthy root systems and top growth only in a soil "alive" with humus, the end product of the decomposition of all organic materials. Later I will give you some practical, valuable information on testing the soil for nutrients and pH. Here I will describe the standard test used to determine soil texture.

If your garden area is small, probably a single test will be sufficient. But if you have extensive shrub border and flower bed areas, I suggest that you take test samples from various places. There can be considerable difference between soils from different areas in a single landscape. Take one-fourth cup of soil from a test area, place it in a quart jar along with a pint of water. Cap the jar tightly and shake it to mix the water and soil thoroughly. Set it aside until all of the soil particles have settled. Don't be in a hurry, it may take the clay particles several days to settle.

Upon examination, you will find the coarse sand on the bottom of the jar. The next layer will be fine sand, followed by silt and, on top, clay. Disregard the bits of organic matter that may be floating on top of the water. If the sand (coarse and fine together) amounts to half the total solids in the jar, you have soil with a light sandy texture. If there is little clay but over half silt, the texture is classified as heavy silt. A clay texture is about one fourth clay with a large amount of silt. The ideal soil for rhododendrons and most garden plants is loam, which contains two parts each of sand and silt and one part of clay.

BETTY WORMALD, *an Award of Merit which is giving her cousin, 'Pink Pearl', a good race for popularity. Resembles 'Marinus Koster' which is not quite as tall growing and a little more spreading. A red bud rises almost ten inches to a conical spire before the flowers fully open. Excellent for the South.*

ROMANY CHAL, *a good red brought out more forcefully by the interesting dark leaves. The new foliage is indumented and some of this characteristic is retained the year around. Successfully grown in warm areas.*

COVER CROPPING AND FIELD COMPOSTING

Because I know how important it is to have the finest possible soil to grow rhododendrons, soil filled with ample organic matter and humus, I will make some additional suggestions about cover cropping and field composting a new property. I will also pass along a few ideas about using vegetative compost from the garden, in the soil of rhododendron beds or as a mulch. This soil conditioning can be done right in the bed that is being established or in a convenient spot and moved later to the bed.

Since it is a rather simple matter to add nutrients to your soil by the use of chemical fertilizers, I will not stress nitrogen producing cover crops such as legumes. I believe it is more important to tell you how to add

LUCKY STRIKE, *one of Mr. Van Veen's finer hybrids. Exceptionally heavy flower substance providing for long-lasting color. Performs well in warm climates but does best in shade. Use very little fertilizer.*

organic matter to the soil by cover-cropping with grasses. For early spring or fall sowing, I suggest rye and rye grass because they are outstanding producers of organic material. If you plan a warm weather sowing of grass for organic build-up, use millet or sudan grass, which will produce a heavy yield in a short time. They can be planted as late as July in most parts of the country. It is a good idea to fertilize the grass crops in order to obtain maximum growth. If you use the soil the following year, you will "salvage" much of this fertilizer.

Field composting consists of turning under a layer of leaves and other plant refuse spread over the ground. Work fertilizer and, if possible, some manure into the soil at the same time. While these materials are decomposing, the grass cover crop can be grown

and then tilled under. Field composting with a rotary tiller or other mechanized equipment requires less work and does a better job than spading, especially if you are reconditioning a large area.

It would be difficult to find a yard so small that it will not produce some soil-building material from its refuse. Wherever plants grow, there is certain to be organic waste available for field composting or to build a compost pile. A sizeable quantity will accumulate in a year's time. There are grass

RUBY BOWMAN, *a burst of prettiness in the garden. A new introduction by John Druecker which is very highly regarded and destined to be a top-rated commercial variety. Will stand the sun very well.*

SPOT COMPOSTING

Try these ideas for making compost for your rhododendrons. Place a six inch layer of trimmings, leaves and other organic material in a five foot square. Never layer grass clippings or leaves too thickly or solidly, or it will prevent the easy flow-through of air and moisture needed for the decomposition process. The pile should be started on a level piece of ground; a ten foot square concrete surface is even better. The base of the pile should only be five feet square, but the extra space will facilitate turning the pile. As it is built, slope the sides like a pyramid.

Place a two inch layer of manure over the first layer of waste plant matter. Cover this with a thin layer of topsoil and then, if the soil is not alkaline, add a sprinkling of lime. If manure is not available, commercial "compost maker" can be used in the quantities

ANNA ROSE WHITNEY, *a variety to own if only for the attractive foliage. A rapid grower which has performed very well in the Southeast.*

KLUIS SENSATION, *a corner of beauty suitable for any landscape. Will withstand much punishment in the form of poor cultural treatment. Also it can take a great amount of sun, but the flowers will last longer in the shade. Mass plantings are effective.*

clippings, leaves, foliage trimmed from plants and spent annuals, to name a few. Properly composted, these materials will save you dollars and your rhododendrons will thrive on the humus they supply.

recommended by the manufacturer. Now the layering should be repeated: six inches of organic matter, two inches of manure, the topsoil and sprinkling of lime. Continue the layering until the pile has reached a height of about five feet. The top layer should cover half the area of the bottom layer and should be concave in order to catch water.

Other than the materials named, three additional principle ingredients are necessary for successful composting: moisture, warmth and air. With a piece of pipe or an old broom handle, punch several holes through the pile from the top. This will permit aeration and an easy flow of water. Sprinkle a little more lime over the pile from time to time. The lime will not greatly affect the pH of an acid soil, but forego the use of lime if the compost will be used in a neutral or alkaline soil.

Keep the composted material moist but not

UNIQUE, a plant habit which bears out the name. A landscape architect's favorite, and highly esteemed for its rounded compactness. Will do well in warm climates but it will require some shade.

A typically American modern landscape demanding low growth and simplicity in design. Neat and compact yellow, 'Unique'; 'Gumpo Pink' Azaleas; versatile 'Blue Diamond'; and the bright, eye-catching 'Jean Marie de Montague.'

KING OF SHRUBS, *the flower will draw attention in any garden. Will do well in warmer climates. Possibly hardier than rated as there is a large plant in the Philadelphia area which never fails to bloom.*

soggy wet. After about four weeks, turn the pile over, mix it well and restack it. Repeat the process monthly until decomposition is complete. The timing will vary because cold temperatures will slow the process of decay.

Here is a simpler means, often used to produce satisfactory compost, although the results are not quite comparable to the first method. Pile the organic material in a four foot square about four feet high. Tramp it down solidly to about three feet in thickness. Sprinkle two pounds of ammonium sulphate over the top. If the vegetable matter is fresh, add a little lime. Be certain that there are no impenetrable layers of grass or leaves. Turn the pile as described above.

There is still another way to handle composting, especially for the gardener who is always neat and orderly. Three well-constructed bins, side by side, can be used with ease and efficiency. The compost material is placed in bin number one. At the first turning time, it is piled into bin number two and

NAOMI GLOW, *one of ten different 'Naomi' clones. The color of these sweet-scented flowers range from pale pink to a rich rose with various undertones of yellow. They resent too much fertilizer.*

JOHN WALTER, *frilled flowers to better reflect the sunlight. A hardy plant of good compactness.*

at the second, into bin number three. With proper timing, it is possible to have compost in various stages of development in all three bins.

USING PERLITE

Perlite is a comparatively new product used for soil improvement, and I recommend it for rhododendrons in beds or containers. This expanded feather-light (when dry) material is volcanic in origin and has proved to be a valuable addition to some soils and container "mixes." It may have a psychological value too. The white granules stand out brightly, as a reminder that you have, indeed, done something to improve the soil. The cost is low, and you may gain a reputation amongst your gardening friends as a "professional" in soil amendment.

COUNTY OF YORK, *this appealing white truss is pale chartreuse in bud. Joe Gable originally called it 'Catalode' after the parents, 'Catawbiense Album' and 'Loderi King George', which contributed hardiness and vigorous growth. The flowers have a heavy satiny substance, and the leaves of older plants will reach up to a foot in length. In young plants the flowers are sometimes partially concealed by the new growth.*

The particles of perlite are studded with minute cavities which retain moisture but store only a certain amount. Excess water drains away quickly since the moisture is not actually absorbed into the particles. Perlite cavities readily release moisture to the plant roots and facilitate movement of air into the soil. These processes are very necessary for healthy root growth.

Perhaps you still have a number of un-answered questions concerning the soil. Because of the complex inter-relationship of soil, fertilizer, moisture, temperature and other factors, you will find some of the answers in later chapters where I give additional details. Incidentally, some excellent pamphlets are available from the U. S. Department of Agriculture, state agricultural colleges and county agents on soils, fertilizers, soil conditioning and drainage.

CHAPTER SIX

Rhododendrons And Moisture

There is an old saying among commercial greenhouse growers: "Never let an inexperienced person get hold of the hose." I cite this to show the importance of watering rhododendrons or any other plant correctly. Commercial growers know that how, when, and the amount of watering largely determines the success of the crop. Without water, all activity ceases in a plant. Water is needed to dissolve nutrients in the soil, to move these nutrients into the root hairs of the plant, to translocate materials within the plant, to provide plant turgidity, and to make transpiration possible.

Nearly all of us occasionally have been guilty of thinking that watering is a simple thing. After all, isn't it just a matter of holding the nozzle or setting the sprinkler for an indeterminate period of time? I have learned from my experience as a commercial grower of rhododrons that it takes considerable know-how and some good judgment to get the most value from your dollar's worth of water. Previously, I have mentioned the importance of soils and how best to improve them so you can grow superb rhodies. Did you know that a foot of sand holds less water than a foot of loam; that sandy soil needs more water than loam in order to produce the same amount of growth? Even though rhododendrons are relatively shallow-rooted, they will not flourish in soil which is moist only at the surface. To emphasize the importance of knowing the types of soil and their relationship to moisture, consider the following interesting facts: one inch of water will penetrate to nearly one and one-half feet in coarse sand; one foot in fine sand; three-quarters of one foot in sandy loam; one-half foot in loam, and a little less than one-half foot in clay. Know the soil type or mixture in which your rhododendrons are growing, and apply enough water for thorough penetration.

REGULARITY IS IMPORTANT

If we fail to satisfy the water needs of rhododendrons, we cannot expect steady growth. If the drought is acute, the plants will certainly die. The importance of even moisture is greater when the plants are young and not established. Many home gardeners waste much of the water they apply to their plantings. As you undoubtedly have noticed, a gentle rainfall penetrates the ground and plant life derives full benefit. But when the rain comes down in a torrent, only a portion of it soaks into the ground.

It takes a regular program of watering to replace the moisture lost through transpiration and evaporation on warm, summer days. The wide range of climatic conditions makes it almost impossible to say how much water your rhododendrons will require, but, unusually good soil conditions and perfect

DR. V. H. RUTGERS, *flowers open as a welcome to the garden. Although there is a slight difference in flower color, the foliage is quite similar to 'America'. 'Dr. V. H. Rutgers' has better plant habit, but is not as hardy.*

mulching will reduce the need considerably. To insure finer, more vigorous rhododendrons with lovely, large blooms each spring, be certain that they do not lack moisture at any time during the year.

In order to accomplish its purpose, water must penetrate the soil to the area around the main roots and a little below. I suggest a simple test of your sprinkling system to determine the depth of water penetration during a set period of time. Turn on the sprinkler for half an hour. Then, with your trowel, cut a plug of soil to see how far the moisture has penetrated. From this evidence, you can determine the sprinkling time necessary to reach the desired depth.

Not all growers, commercial or amateur, agree on the frequency of watering rhododendrons or other plants. Some like to water frequently, and this method is acceptable if done correctly. The danger with frequent waterings is the tendency to cut short the duration of each watering period. Often the moisture never soaks down more than three or four inches into the soil. You can avoid underwatering your plants by using the test I suggested above. Personally, I like to moisten the soil deeply each time and water less frequently.

To the question of how often rhododendrons should be watered, I reply, "When they

MRS. A. T. DE LA MARE, *stairsteps of loveliness. The buds are rose pink and the flowers are scented. A plant which is both heat and cold tolerant. Plant on right is a patio scene in British Columbia.*

Clifford A. Fenner

ROCKET, *the unique leaves and habit makes this hybrid from Shammarello a fine landscape plant. Performs well in the sun and warm weather.*

need it." However, never wait until the need is critical! Their moisture requirements are increased or diminished by the amount of rainfall, the type of soil, how well the plants are mulched, the quality of drainage, and other conditions. Too many gardeners tend to overlook the fact that rhododendrons, with their broad leaves, transpire considerably during hot weather. This moisture, lost even in sheltered positions, must be replaced. If you notice scorched patches or margins on the rhododendron leaves during hot weather, they are quite likely due to insufficient amounts of water reaching the root system, rather than to over-fertilization or some other problem. The young, tender growth is especially susceptible to this scorching.

During a spell of hot weather, even though the soil is moist, rhododendron roots may not absorb moisture quickly enough to prevent leaf burning. In an area with infrequent hot weather of short duration, running the sprinkler usually will eliminate this problem. If you grow rhododendrons where the climate is dry and hot, I suggest that you install fine mist-type nozzles which can be in operation over prolonged periods without causing overwatering. I have mentioned that too much water is as detrimental to your rhododendrons as is too little. Watch for puddles which linger after watering, since these indicate improper drainage and the need for its immediate correction by the methods described in the previous chapter.

BLUE PETER, *one of many rhododendrons surrounding the State Capitol Building at Atlanta, Georgia. Many are in full sun most of the day. These plantings were established several years ago under the supervision of Ben W. Fortson, Jr., Secretary of State, Keeper of Building and Grounds.*

METHODS OF APPLICATION

I have seen some well-grown rhododendrons which consistently have been watered by flooding, but I prefer overhead irrigation. I can almost imagine my rhododendron plants smiling as they receive a shower of water over their foliage. Besides providing necessary moisture, the overhead system cleanses the broad leaves of the plants. A great many gardens with uneven terrain, which prevents surface irrigating, are watered easily by rain-like, overhead sprinkling.

What time of day to water? Except during heat waves, I like the early morning hours because more water soaks into the soil and less is lost through evaporation. But there is no reason why you should not water during the heat of the day. I have not experienced any harm to rhododendrons caused

MADAME GUILLEMOT, *a free-flowering, late variety which extends the blooming season well into June. The flowers are long-lasting and hold color well in the sun. Registered as 'Monsieur Guillemot' but generally sold in this country as 'Madame'.*

by irrigating on hot days. If you believe that sprinkling during periods of high temperatures is harmful, avoid watering during the heat of the day, unless you know the plants will be damaged. Do avoid watering in the evening in hot, humid climates. Plants that remain wet throughout a warm night are very susceptible to disease.

My observation is that more rhododendrons are lost in foundation plantings than anywhere else, mainly because of reflected heat and lack of moisture. It is so easy to be fooled during rainy weather when the lawn and open beds are lush and green. We might forget that eaves, balconies and other wide overhangs can reduce the sky-borne moisture considerably, perhaps to none at all.

Even during the winter, many rhododendrons and other foundation plants are damaged by lack of moisture. Broadleaf ever-

CADIS, *the lovely contrast between buds and open flowers is arresting. Joe Gable used 'Caroline' and R. discolor to produce this fragrant, strong grower. Will not bud up well if it has too much shade.*

MISSION BELLS, *one of Ben Lancaster's very fine hybrids. There is fragrance, too. A R. williamsianum hybrid which will stand sun and warm weather quite well.*

greens lose moisture during the winter months through transpiration. If drying winds occur, the loss is greatly increased. My advice is that you give particular attention to rhododendrons covered by an overhang to be certain they receive sufficient moisture through the fall and winter seasons.

The most critical time in a rhododendron's life comes during the first few months after placement. It will adjust better if syringed with water daily for the first week. Starting with a good soaking at the time of planting, ample water should be applied to the root system every third day for the first four or five weeks. During the fall do not give young rhododendrons quite as much moisture as older plants. Overwatering can cause soft growth which is more subject to freeze damage. Your on-the-spot judgment will have to serve as guide in this regard.

SAPPHIRE, *it shines in the proper setting. The foliage has a spicy, aromatic scent. A rock garden shrub which is best grown in the sun. Rhododendron varieties of this type lose their beautiful compactness with too much shade. 'Cutie' is a good companion plant.*

MULCHING AND MOISTURE

If there is any secret to growing rhododendrons successfully, I believe it is closely related to proper mulching procedures. Mulching protects and cools the root area, aids in nutrition, and helps maintain the proper acidity. However, in the case of protection, there is a situation in which a mulch can become a detriment. A mulch restricts the earth's heat from escaping. In the fall, at the time of the first frosts, it often is beneficial to remove the mulch from any young plants in your garden. On frosty mornings, close to the ground, the air temperature can be as much as five degrees lower above mulched surfaces than adjoining unmulched areas. Watering the day before an expected frost will increase the warmth of unmulched earth and further minimize the effects of autumn frosts. You might want to temper the idea somewhat in certain parts of the country, or

CYNTHIA, *over 100 years old and still among the most popular. The two plants pictured are close to 60 years of age. They were moved into the American Rhododendron Society Test Garden in 1950 when they were about 40 years old. 'Cynthia' will grow almost anywhere under the most trying of conditions. She can be cut to the ground and will come back vigorously.*

perhaps disregard it altogether, if there is little danger from fall frosts. Keep in mind that many of the rhododendron's roots are quite close to the soil surface and some may, indeed, be in the mulch itself. So perform this task carefully and again apply the mulch as winter's cold sets in.

As sometimes happens, not all of the rhododendron experts agree on the best mulching materials or on the proper procedure. These differences, I am sure, often arise because of the variations in cultural situations,

ROSE ELF, *one of the delightful little fellows the garden needs. Ben Lancaster introduced this hybrid. A free-flowering, low grower which will take full exposure.*

climatic conditions, availability of mulching materials, and other factors. Perhaps all the experts are right, considering the circumstances.

I have cautioned you against planting rhododendrons too deeply, especially in heavy soils. Shallow planting is recommended but it can cause problems of leaf drop and winter frost heaving unless you apply a mulch. The mulch also prevents cracking of the soil which sometimes damages a rhododendron's delicate roots. However, gardeners appreciate mulches mostly because they suppress weed growth!

FABIA, *in several forms and colors of terra-cotta, crimson, apricot-orange, orange-pink and orange. Ideally, this variety should be planted where one can look up into the hanging flowers and observe the tawny indumentum beneath the felted leaves.*

ELIZABETH, *this handsome red-red goes well with azaleas in landscape. In warm areas it flowers in the fall, but it is so free flowering that these blooms are never missed in the spring. 'Elizabeth' seems to grow rapidly the first few years and then she slows down. Possibly this is caused by the heavy flowering. She does not like too much fertilizer or alkaline water. Performs well in warm weather climates.*

I prefer to use organic mulches for several reasons. They promote the formation of colloids, glue-like substances which help meter nutrients to the plants. Organic mulches improve water balance in the soil, increasing water-retention capacity and permitting a steady moisture flow into the root system. Be cautious of increasing the water retention of heavy soils without providing extra drainage. As organic mulches decompose, they improve granulation of the soil and aeration and also add humus.

Temperature, air and moisture influence the decay rate of a mulch. I urge you to

watch the nutrient balance of mulched soils. Many materials, especially bark and sawdust, tend to pull nitrogen and phosphorus levels down as bacteria decompose the mulch. Although the use of mulches has some influence on acidity, no harmful change in pH is apt to occur. Organisms in the soil are increased by mulching, as is the supply and activity of earthworms. Some mulches may tend to increase certain disease organisms, but the possibility is too remote to cause concern under normal garden conditions.

When choosing a mulch, consider the cost, availability, fire hazard, frost protection, weed seed content, acidity and rodent appeal. Do not overlook the appearance of a mulch material in your garden. Rhodies deserve an attractive foil to display their handsome blooms and foliage. I like barkdust, partially rotted sawdust or coarse Douglas Fir sawdust for use on rhododendron plantings in the Pacific Northwest. Douglas Fir wood chips or shavings also give good service and appearance and are readily available.

SPRING DAWN, *could spring dawn with more splendor? An early blooming Shammarello hybrid. It seems to be quite tolerant of the growing conditions in the Midwest.*

Pine needles, oak leaves, spent hops and beech leaves are recommended mulching materials. The looser sorts can be piled more deeply around the plants than the finer kinds. Sawdust is best used about three inches deep. While I find our Northwest softwood sawdust ideal for mulching rhododendrons, I suggest experimenting a bit before covering all of a rhododendron planting with hardwood and other sawdusts. It is better to hurt a plant or two than the entire landscape. Although peat moss has a pleasant appearance and other good qualities, the crust it forms will shed light rainfall and sprinkling. Avoid tobacco stems and, possibly, cocoa shells for mulching. Their potassium content is so heavy that rhododendrons may be injured.

Perhaps you have not thought about using ground cover plants as a living mulch in a rhododendron planting. I recommend them

AZOR, for salmon pink color, here's a real winner. Best grown in the shade as a background plant because of a somewhat sparse habit. Try 'Fabia' in front.

PARSONS GLORIOSUM, a century old ironclad still in the trade. Excellent full plant which will do equally well in sun or shade.

highly. They offer little competition for nutrients, protect the soil, reduce maintenance, and provide a harmonious setting for the rhodies. To protect both the rhododendrons and the small ground plants, keep the area well mulched with barkdust or any suitable mulch material until a dense cover develops. There are a number of ground cover and other attractive plants which grow well amongst rhododendrons. Among them are: *Ajuga reptans* (Bugle-weed); *Epimedium* species; creeping *Euonymus Fortunei* varieties (Wintercreeper); *Gaultheria procumbens* (Wintergreen); dwarf *Hosta* species (Plantain-lily); *Myosotis scorpioides* (True

ELIE, *glistening foliage and beautiful pink coloring join hands. Judicious shearing is sometimes necessary to keep this vigorous grower in bounds. Endowed with generous foliage it will make a pleasingly formal, compact plant.*

R. KEISKEI, *lemon-lime charm is delightful in fenced garden. Almost every growth terminal will set a bud. There are two forms available, this dwarf and the taller grower.*

Forget-me-not) ; *Pachistima Canbyi* (Rat-Stripper) ; *Pachysandra terminalis* (Japanese Spurge) ; *Primula species* (Primroses) ; *Ranunculus montanus* (Mountain Buttercup) ; *Vinca minor* (Periwinkle or Myrtle) ;

Viola species (Violets) ; *Waldsteinia fragarioides* (Barren-strawberry) and others. Avoid vigorous, twining vines, such as ivies, which may eventually spoil the beauty of your rhodies by smothering them in luxuriant foliage.

ODEE WRIGHT, *you will find it hard to pass up this rich yellow. A new introduction by Arthur Wright which should join the "most popular" class in a very few years.*

MARS *and* COUNTY OF YORK, *a captivating study in contrast. While both plants are quite hardy, 'Mars' will do best in afternoon shade. 'County of York' being a faster grower should be planted in the background.*

CHAPTER SEVEN

They Thrive On Proper Feeding

The title of this chapter is not meant to imply that rhododendrons require a great deal of fertilizer. Under normal circumstances, they do not. Much of their nutrients come from the breakdown of natural materials in the soil through the symbiotic association of bacteria and rhododendrons. There are some experts who say that rhododendrons need no fertilizer at all. I will examine this idea in relation to my personal experiences.

The function of soil is very complex and the soil scientists continue to learn more about it. Actually, soil, as we usually define it, is not necessary to produce rhododendrons and azaleas or other plants. The well-publicized California container mixes, which consist of various combinations of sand and peat moss or bark dust, illustrate this point. But grown in such mixtures, plants do need fertilizer. I have seen some fine rhododendrons and azaleas produced in containers with only pure peat moss as the growing medium. They would have died for want of nutrients without controlled feeding. We use true soil for reasons of economy, and because it usually is in abundant supply.

BACTERIA'S ROLE

The soil system embodies physical, chemical and biological factors. Given some assistance from the gardener, these three soil factors work together to produce the conditions necessary for good plant growth. The biological factor includes bacteria (some minute and others of greater size), algae, molds, protozoan, nematodes, worms and roots. Bacteria in the soil make compounds and elements available to plants by converting otherwise unusable forms into readily available food. Bacteria and nutrients form in the soil a remarkable partnership which benefits the plants growing there.

Even though some micro-organisms can exist in air-dry soil for long periods of time, it takes moist conditions to make them active and useful in your garden soil. Maximum bacterial activity usually occurs when the soil moisture stands at about 50 per cent of capacity. Most bacteria converts the nitrogen of the soil into a form usable by plants, although some bacteria are nitrogen-fixers. The latter type has the ability to take nitrogen from the air and place it in the soil in a form plants can use.

Carbon-filled materials such as peat, leafmold, manure and other organic matter are needed for the functioning of bacteria. When excessive amounts of nitrogen have been consumed in the decay of sawdust, straw and similar materials worked into the soil, the micro-organisms compete with the plants for any remaining nitrogen. If the amount of organic materials is very great, the micro-organisms also compete for the phosphorus. Bacterial activity is at its peak when the soil

great concern to the gardener. It is the re-arrangement of ions in the soil when new elements are introduced through the use of fertilizer. Until this exchange process and the bacterial needs are satisfied, your plants receive none of the fertilizer added to the soil. According to an old axiom, "First you fertilize the soil and then the crops." Of course, the bacteria repay you by making food available to your plants.

Organisms decompose organic matter and, in the process, release nutrients usable to plants. All the elements rhododendrons need for growth can be present in the soil but of no value if these elements are in a form the plants cannot assimilate. While the organic matter is being decomposed, bacteria are multiplying and dying. The organic plant materials and the dead bacteria decay at varying rates; a portion of each is left to de-compose at a slower pace. Lignin is one of

R. CAMPYLOGYNUM, *truest of hanging bells. This species is the cremastum form which will reach a height of two feet. Place high in a rock garden to better see the flowers and in a position to see the reflection of the sun through the bells. This is also a good Bonsai plant.*

ELSE FRYE, *an ideal plant for the redwood container on a deck. However, this requires considerable pruning effort. More naturally 'Else Frye' might be trained as an espalier. The four-inch flowers are fragrant and of good substance.*

temperature is about 85 degrees Fahrenheit, although some activity will continue down to freezing and up to 100 degrees or more.

The addition of fertilizers to the soil spurs bacterial activity. In most cases, a "bal-anced" or complete fertilizer is desirable. Tied in with the activity of the many kinds of bacteria is the exchange capacity of the soil, a technical subject which need not be of the results of these processes, and is slow to break down. These many products in combination form humus, a substance vital for all successful plant growth.

IMPORTANCE OF CORRECT pH

Closely associated with good results in the growing of rhododendrons is soil pH, or in this case the soil acidity. There is probably nothing more confusing to the average home gardener than the subject of pH, and perhaps I can clear up some of the misunderstanding. Actually pH is not complicated. Technically, it means the percentage of hydrogen ions concentrated in the soil. Scientists, realizing that acidity or alkalinity influences plant growth, devised the pH scale as a simple means of testing the soil acidity or alkalinity. On this scale, which is graded from 4 to 9, 7.0 is neutral. All readings below 7.0 are acid and those above are alkaline.

CARITA, *tough foliage which will hold up with exposure to wind, but will not do well with too much sun. A worthwhile plant in the landscape for foliage and low habit.*

MRS. BERNICE BAKER, *the highlights of pure beauty. One of H. L. Larson's new hybrids which might be hard to find. The interesting flower markings reflect light very well.*

R. YAKUSIMANUM, *probably the finest of them all. Discovered a few years ago on a mountain top of the small island of Yaku Shima near Japan. A beautifully proportioned little shrub with thick, velvety indumentum.*

On the left is the F.C.C. form recently named 'Koichiro Wada', after the famous Japanese nurseryman who discovered the plant. On the right is a selected form, 'Mist Maiden', a little faster growing plant.

The pH range of 6.0 to 6.5 is best for the majority of home gardens because it is within this range that many of the fertilizer elements are most available. For rhododendrons, however, the best pH range is from 4.5 to 5.5. They will perform quite well, though not at their best, in soils that have a pH of 6.0. Do not try rhodies in soils above a pH of 6.0 until you have amended it to a lower pH reading. There are some soils which will register a pH lower than 4.5, though they are rare, and their pH can be raised. It is acceptable to compromise a bit on the pH, if you wish to grow rhododendrons with other shrubs and plants.

How does a gardener adjust the pH? It is really quite simple, but he must begin by taking a soil sample for testing. I have told many people about soil testing, perhaps without realizing that the method of taking a soil sample needs some explanation. Unless the sample is taken carefully and precisely, the test will be useless.

PINK PEARL, *anthers curl appealingly around the pistil. A very well known variety which received an Award of Merit in 1897. Does well in sun and warm weather areas.*

Don Gray

ROSEUM SUPERBUM, *a good plant similar to 'Roseum Elegans'. A free-growing variety which is quite full. An excellent screen or background plant, particularly for subzero areas.*

CHRISTMAS CHEER, *well-mounded plant brings beauty to the home in March. In mild weather it will open much earlier. Frequently used in early forcing but some color is lost. Will stand a considerable amount of sun. Sometimes confused with 'Rosamundi' which is larger leaved and a darker pink.*

SOIL SAMPLING

Never mix portions from different kinds of soils. Instead, take a separate sample wherever there is a marked change in soil texture, depth, slope, degree of drainage, management history or, in some cases, color. In most instances, a gardener's property contains about the same soil throughout. However, as I pointed out earlier, there can be differences, especially at the site of a new home where the topsoil and subsoil have been interchanged or mixed.

Remove all extraneous matter from the soil surface before taking a sample. Then dig a six-inch-deep, V-shaped hole with a spade or trowel. Remove a one-inch slice of soil from one side of the hole. Remove and discard the edges of the slice, until the sample is about one inch thick, one or two inches wide, and six inches deep. Put it in a clean bucket or box. Your testing will be more accurate if you take eight or ten samples from

MRS. TOM H. LOWINSKY, *with a prominent blotch on recurved, ivory white petals, these flowers might be described as "Orchid-like". Although an older variety, it is new in this country. Does very well in the warm weather of Texas.*

JANET BLAIR, *the four-inch scented flowers are among the largest available for cold climates. A vigorous plant which is about as wide as it is high.*

the same area and mix them thoroughly. If you are satisfied that soil types and conditions are the same throughout your yard, take samples from various parts and mix them well. About one pint of the mixed soil is required for testing. It is best to take samples when the soil is moist but not wet. Then air-dry the soil but never use artificial heat.

Some excellent do-it-yourself soil testing kits are available to test the pH of your soil as well as the principal fertilizer elements. Directions are quite easy to follow.

Soil testing can be done in the soil testing laboratory of your state university. Get

J. H. VAN NES, *beautiful texture and glowing flower. Fertilize this variety very lightly. The flowers are exceptionally long-lasting.*

available literature and containers for the samples from your county agent. Completely fill the container and be sure that the package is wrapped and tied securely. Each state charges a small fee for the service, but it is well worth the cost.

MAKING pH ADJUSTMENTS

When you know the pH of your soil, how do you make any needed adjustments? To lower the pH (make the soil more acid), use an acid-type fertilizer and an acid mulch, such as oakleaf mold or peat moss. Actually, the mulch has only a minor influence on the pH. Sulphur really is the best way to reduce pH, because it acts slowly and is long-lasting. It must be used *before* planting! The amount will depend upon the alkalinity of the soil. I suggest from one to two pounds per 100

HELENE SCHIFFNER, *the purest white, and just look at its golden anthers! Interesting black buds before opening. Since dead white produces a dull effect try planting in front of a large pink.*

LITTLE GEM, *truly a gem with well-set magnificent foliage. A rockery addition which is best planted high in order to see the sun through the blooms.*

SPRING GLORY, *its trusses stand upright to command attention. A hardy new introduction by Mr. Shammarello. Holds up well in sun or shade.*

square feet in most instances. Six to eight weeks will pass before any effect will be noticeable in the soil pH. I normally recommend the use of 1¼ cups of iron sulphate per 100 square feet each spring as an acidifying supplement.

Do not panic if you suddenly learn that your soil is not acid enough for optimum results with rhododendrons. Although the "special" acid fertilizers will not harm your plants, there seldom is any real need for them. Ammonium sulphate, which tends to make the soil more acid, is contained in many complete balanced fertilizers and is ideal for rhododendrons. It provides the ammonium form of nitrogen rather than the nitrate form, which can raise the pH. Use one pound of ammonium sulphate per 100 square feet to help acidify the soil, and water it in well. A second application may be needed four to six weeks later. A complete fertilizer should be applied at the rate recommended by the manufacturer.

Either hydrated lime or agricultural lime can be used to raise the pH of extremely acid soil. Hydrated lime acts faster but is not as safe or long-lasting as agricultural lime. Either of these materials should be used at the rate of two to three pounds per 100 square feet of soil to raise the pH by one point.

Is there any other way than testing to determine the soil pH? No, you will not learn a thing by looking, smelling, feeling or tasting. I suggest summer testing of areas you intend to plant in the fall, and in the fall, checking beds you plan to use in the spring. This will give you an opportunity to condition the soil before setting out the plants. It is a good idea to continue a regular schedule of soil testing each year, if pH and fertility

PINNACLE, *peak of beauty is seen in these trusses. Perhaps the hardiest of the Shammarello hybrids. A good plant for most any growing condition.*

MOONSTONE, *positively one of the finest of the semi-dwarf yellows. Better planted away from a frosty pocket which might nip the early new young growth. Some shade is best for flower color.*

troubles persist. You may be surprised to learn that the pH and nutrient supply can change considerably over a period of years. This is particularly true in areas with alkaline water.

To help offset the effect of alkaline water, the soil should be as acid as your rhododendrons and other shrubs will tolerate. As you continue to irrigate, the pH will be raised by the alkaline content of the water. The pH of a heavy soil will remain more stable, within limits, because it readily absorbs highly soluble salts without injury to the plants. On the other hand, the pH of a sandy soil will increase rapidly under the same conditions.

ORGANIC AND INORGANIC FERTILIZERS

Organic fertilizers are ideal for rhododendrons, from the standpoint of both nutrients and humus. Cottonseed meal, castor pomace

85

LEO, *fancy this lovely rich ball of red crowning a rhodie in your yard. Up to 24 waxy florets to a truss. A wonderful plant in the woodland.*

plant growth. The combination may differ from one area to another, to compensate for varying soil and other conditions. You will have to rely on the fertilizer manufacturers to supply the correct formula. If you believe that a standard mixture is not helping your rhododendrons or other plants, you can request a special formulation or mix your own basic ingredients. However, the problem is probably the result of other factors.

The balanced fertilizer you buy will contain three principal ingredients: nitrogen, phosphorus and potash, and the percentages of each will be printed on the container, always in that order. This is a legal requirement. Everything else in the bag is "filler" of no special use to your plants, or minor elements. Knowing this should help you select a fertilizer best suited to your requirements. Always check the amounts of nitro-

or soybean meal are beneficial to rhodies and other broad-leaved evergreens. My friend, David Leach, recommends one-half cup of cottonseed meal mixed with the back-fill soil used around the root area when planting a new rhododendron and watering it in thoroughly. He also suggests the use of an iron chelate fertilizer to guard against iron deficiency (chlorosis).

The term "balanced" or "complete" fertilizer, with the designations 20-20-20, 6-10-4, 5-3-2 and the like, can be confusing to an amateur gardener. In brief, a balanced or complete fertilizer contains the right proportions of the principal elements for good

GRAF ZEPPELIN, *the lighter-than-air machine was never as pretty as this! Just look at this handsome ball-shaped truss. A newer Dutch hybrid becoming ever more popular.*

Oklahoma City is the setting for this specimen plant of 'Mrs. E. C. Stirling.' With proper care in the selection of varieties, many can be grown successfully in the more difficult areas of the Americas.

Barney Hillerman

DISCA, *a beautiful frilled white which is delightful to smell. This is the reverse cross of the pink 'Cadis', R. discolor x 'Caroline'. Performs best in light shade.*

gen, phosphorus and potash, plus any minor elements which are included. Most soils contain enough minor elements for vigorous plant growth. Never waste money on fertilizers with minor elements unless your soil really needs them.

Understanding the effects of the main elements on your rhododendrons can be an aid to feeding them correctly. Nitrogen, applied in the right amount, will promote normal growth and healthy green leaves. Too much nitrogen will "burn" the foliage, destroy young feeder roots, and force excessive vegetative growth.

Superphosphate is the chief source of phosphorus used by most gardeners. It promotes root development and increases flower production. Without ample phosphorus, the quality and quantity of blooms is reduced. Several years ago, the late Arthur S.

Myhre conducted experiments in nutrition with rhododendrons. An important finding showed that ample phosphorus produces excellent bud set and high quality, well-colored flowers. The phosphorus should be applied in late winter or very early spring. A recommended method is to punch a few holes with a broomhandle or similar implement, three or four inches deep, around the perimeter of the rhodie foliage. This distance usually coincides with the outer ends of the feeding roots. Fill the holes with superphosphate. The plant will then have all the phosphorous it needs for maximum healthy growth and bloom production.

Potassium has over-all value to plants, providing them with greater vigor and disease resistance. Rhododendrons without suf-

MRS. CHARLES S. SARGENT, *a real ironclad, one which will survive 25 degree below temperatures. Good as a screen or in mass plantings.*

Don Gray

ficient potassium will look unhealthy, and their appearance will disappoint you.

Some gardeners believe that rhododendrons and azaleas should be fertilized with compounds formulated especially for them. I believe this depends to a great extent on your particular soil and growing conditions. Since most fertilizers are compounded to get the best results from the total garden, there is the possibility that some balanced fertilizers may leave an alkaline residue. If a particular formulation does do this, it will increase the alkalinity problem in growing rhododendrons, azaleas and other acid-loving plants. I believe that this is a matter of concern in very few instances. If it is, by all means use a fertilizer designed especially for acid-soil plants.

WHEN TO FEED RHODODENDRONS

The quantity and quality of the flowers on your rhododendrons next year depends greatly on what and when you feed them this year. True, most plants will produce a few inferior flowers, whether fed or not. If you desire the best from your prize rhodies, you will obtain it only by giving them attention at the proper time. Even a small amount of fertilizer at the right time will produce

Autumn Gold, *a distinctive color break not found in any other rhodie. Luxurious if grown in slight shade. A Van Veen introduction.*

89

Thousands of young rhododendrons in full sun in one of the Van Veen commercial growing grounds in the Willamette Valley south of Portland, Oregon. Notice the overhead sprinklers operating in the background. An airplane is used for dusting and spraying.

lovelier bloom than a great amount at the wrong time.

The colorful flowers on your rhododendrons in the spring began with bud initiation the previous summer. The fertilizer you gave the plants that spring gave them the boost they needed to produce those many plump buds during the summer.

As I mentioned before, the three essential food elements for all plants, flowering or otherwise, are nitrogen, phosphorus and potassium. Improper fertilizer balance can promote growth at the expense of bud and flower development. I believe that you are interested in both healthy, attractive plants and an abundance of well-formed flowers.

Nitrogen, though necessary and beneficial, tends to slow down flower development and keep the plants from maturing. Too much

nitrogen for rhododendrons, and certain other broad-leaf evergreens, promotes excellent foliage growth but curtails development of flower buds.

Is the answer, then, that nitrogen should be neglected in favor of phosphorus and potassium to promote better flower production? Not at all. All three elements are needed to keep the plant growth in proper balance. If you feed only part of the three essential chemicals, you will notice a steady decline in the appearance, vigor and performance of your rhododendrons.

My suggestion is that you use a balanced fertilizer, such as 5-10-10, at the rate of three or four ounces per square yard, or about three pounds per 100 square feet. Feeding should be done in early to midspring, preferably before late April. Later feeding has a tendency to promote growth which will not have time to harden off before cold weather comes along. Soft, succulent growth is the first to be damaged by a freeze. The plants need to be in a mature, woody condition from top to bottom when fall and cold weather arrive.

My recommendation for feeding rhododendrons is to be a bit skimpy with fertilizer. In fact, I have friends who advise not to feed rhododendrons except to amend an unfavorable pH situation or to correct a developing chlorosis. The plants do get much of their needed nutrition from the decomposition of

DAVID GABLE, *well-set trusses go with the fine habit of this variety. Note red-throated pink flowers which are fully four inches in diameter. Mr. Gable feels that this is one of his best. He first called it 'Pink No. 1'. Actually this hybrid was so good that he never assigned any more numbers to that particular batch of seedlings.*

Don Gray

R. IMPEDITUM, *what better way to beautify the foot of a rock wall? A reliable, hardy species which is ideal for the rock garden, border, or in a mass planting. Forms a neat, compact mound when grown in full sun.*

mulch material and humus in the soil. You may have a friend or neighbor who is doing a good job of growing rhododendrons. Perhaps he will share his knowledge with you. Practically everyone who grows rhodies has his own ideas for achieving best results. I always listen when I am with people who are discussing rhododendrons. It is always possible to learn new tricks from their experiences!

Deficiency of a particular soil element may cause poor plant growth. If you can determine what element is involved, you can easily amend your fertilizing program and correct the deficiency. In the next chapter I pass along many tips about preventing and curing problems that may affect your rhododendrons. Fortunately they are naturally long-lived and trouble-free.

CHAPTER EIGHT

Preventing Problems

 Rhododendrons are, in my opinion, the most beautiful of all broad-leaved evergreen shrubs grown in American gardens. They offer the widest range of flower colors, foliage interest and habits of growth, and they make a tremendous contribution to a landscape at all seasons of the year. Because of their great diversity, they are a fascinating life-long hobby for plant collectors, and happily, they are mostly free of serious diseases, insect pests and other problems!

"An ounce of prevention is worth a pound of cure." Following this wise adage can help you breeze through your rhododendron gardening experiences without any serious problems. In this chapter I discuss ways to prevent troubles and to cure those that might occur now and then.

Are you familiar with proper garden sanitation? Never allow debris to accumulate in and near your garden. Slugs, snails, cut worms, earwigs, and symphyllids are some of the most destructive pests which hide beneath old boards, flats, flower pots and other objects left on the ground.

Plant diseases and some insects, too, are encouraged by poor air circulation in the garden. Weeds provide a natural hiding place for insects and rodents, so keep weeds down in and adjacent to your garden. Insects breed rapidly among the weeds and then move to your garden plants. Some insects, such as aphids, which feed on diseased weeds, often transmit diseases to your plants.

Although poor color and lack of vitality in your plants can be a sign of insect invasion or disease problems, they are not necessarily the cause. A starving plant, one which is over-fed, one suffering from poor air circulation, one receiving insufficient light or too much light, can also exhibit some of the symptoms caused by pests and disease.

It has been said that you should never look a gift horse in the mouth, but I say you should examine thoroughly any rhododendron or other plant before you put it into your garden. Whenever you accept gift plants, you should be certain that they are free from insects and diseases. Many of these pests will move from one kind of plant to another. We have learned that a plant pest, such as the Japanese Beetle, indigenous to a distant part of the world, thrives all too well here. Accidentally, we have imported some really "mean" kinds.

STAY WITH THE DIRECTIONS

Painstaking research has been carried on by the U.S.D.A. and state experimental stations, as well as the manufacturers, to make certain that the agricultural chemicals you buy are safe and effective when properly used, and I stress that word "properly." Whenever you use any of these chemicals, follow directions very carefully. The conclusions of the chemical companies are the results of extensive research. The warnings printed on the labels must not be taken lightly. If the manufacturer warns the user to avoid breathing the material or to avoid skin

RAINBOW, *an artist would be hard pressed to paint it more attractively. A profuse bloomer on a plant that grows as wide as it is high.*

control. Very often it takes a specific chemical, although some materials will control several kinds of insects or diseases. Use contact sprays on sucking insects such as aphids, thrips, scale insects in the crawling stage and leaf hoppers. Among the contact sprays are diazinon, lindane, malathion, nicotine and rotenone. It is good practice, wherever possible, to stay with those materials which

What better way to greet a visitor at the door than with rhododendrons. Artistic shaping for a specific use as done so well at this California home often can be more effective than the formal, perfectly rounded plant.

Charles Kassler

contact, follow those instructions precisely. Believe the label directions about mixing the correct proportions. It always bothers me to see rhododendrons or other plants needlessly damaged because a well-meaning gardener either guessed at the amount of chemical he was mixing in his sprayer, or decided that if a "little" is good for the plants, a "lot" would certainly be better. Dosages have been carefully determined by expert research. Using more than recommended usually causes plant damage, and using less results in poor control. Certain pests, such as mites, often survive and become resistant to the chemical. Future spraying with the same chemical will have little or no effect on them. I have found many times that a gardener's complaint about a spray's unsatisfactory control of a pest or disease resulted from improper dosage or poor application.

Use the pesticide or fungicide which is recommended for the problem you are trying to

SNOW LADY, *spring's suggestion of winter. This hybrid is extremely heat tolerant. Being an early bloomer, the buds will need protection from frost in some areas.*

are less apt to cause human or plant injury. For this reason I like to use a rotenone-based spray against aphids and some other insects. I realize this isn't always possible, and sometimes a gardener must resort to strong measures to obtain the desired results. Insects can sap the life from a plant, which can do nothing in its own defense. The gardener must come to the rescue.

Pesticides used for the chewing type of insects kill by paralysis or by fumigant action. Lindane, DDT, methoxychlor and lead arsenates are some of the preferred ones. May I suggest that you bypass DDT, at least until

TIDBIT, *you will consider it a feast for the eyes. A unique hybrid by the late Rudolph Henny. Prefers shade and must have excellent drainage.*

Clifford A. Fenner

PINK PETTICOATS, *a stunning new pink for the land-scape. The frills increase the florescence when the sun is reflected through the huge blooms.*

we learn more about the problems of land and water pollution it seems to be causing. Although it has been and still is at this writing an approved chemical, more and more evidence is piling up against DDT. Whenever you use the arsenates, guard against the possibility of children and pets coming in contact with the material by brushing against wet plants or inhaling the spray or dust in the air.

Concerning other precautions, do you keep your garden chemicals under lock and key? You should. There have been too many incidents with horrible consequences of children consuming garden chemicals. And never put any sort of garden chemical into anything but its original container. Perhaps you read of the man who picked up a coke bottle and took one small taste of its contents. He spat it out immediately and rinsed out his mouth. He died a few minutes later. The coke bottle contained a powerful, deadly, spray concentrate. Should you accidentally get any garden chemical on your skin, immediately wash it off with soap and water. And if you are concerned about the effects of that chemical or develop any symptom of illness, call a doctor without delay.

Among the many chemicals used to control diseases which attack plants are ferbam, captan, zineb, fermate and maneb. Many soil pests can be controlled with soil insecticides such as lindane, used like a liquid fertilizer, or chlordane dust.

PREVENTION IS THE ANSWER

Spring is probably the most welcome season of the year, especially to the gardener. After a winter of dormancy, it is wonderful to see the swelling buds and growing grass and to hear the chirping birds. The home gardener finds himself "champing at the bit" in pleasurable anticipation of restoring his yard to full beauty.

You and your plants are not the only survivors of winter; a great many kinds of insects and diseases have a l s o wintered through and are ready to start "dining" on your plants as soon as spring comes.

The alert gardener will start control measures early each spring and continue a regular program throughout the summer and fall. I am a great believer in prevention and almost all garden problems can be prevented.

Understanding the organisms and conditions which cause problems for rhododendrons and other plants will help the gardener prevent problems. A plant does not get sick without a cause. Environment has a big

IDEALIST, *one of the most beautiful rhododendrons ever grown. Possibly more hardy than rated. Slight shade is recommended.*

influence and involves soil, drainage, aeration, temperature, fertilizer and tilth. When these are out of balance, trouble will ensue. I have pointed out in other chapters the relationships between all these factors and a healthy plant.

Injuries to plants cause many unnecessary problems. Some are caused by man and the equipment he uses as he works around his plants. All care should be exercised to prevent damaging branches, bark, foliage and

MRS. HORACE FOGG, *take a second look at the deep throat color in that large-sized truss. Good performer in sun and warm climates. Do not fertilize too heavily.*

DAPHNOIDES, *truly adorned is this home's corner with medium-height plant. A unique landscape piece which is really different. One is reminded of "Pittosporum." A slow grower and remarkably hardy.*

CRIMSON GLORY, *a vibrant red with lovely frilling. Unfortunately, the original source and parentage of this variety is not known. Use in the background because older plants become somewhat open.*

roots. Pests and diseases often gain entry through such wounds and those injuries caused by freeze damage.

Viruses multiply in living tissue only. They are microscopic in size and usually are transmitted from one plant to another by insects. If you control the insects, you control

most of the viruses. Of course, they can be spread from a diseased plant to a healthy one by the careless use of pruners. And some harmful viruses may be present in the soil.

Bacteria are 1/50,000 of an inch in size, and they reproduce by fission. Earlier I tell you about the beneficial bacteria of the soil, but there are some "bad guys," too. The fabulous power of reproduction possessed by bacteria would enable one bacterium, under completely optimum conditions, to produce twelve tons of bacteria in twenty-four hours. Bacteria can be introduced through a wound, transmitted by people and animals or moisture in the air. They usually disseminate by the water in the soil.

Fungi measure 1/25,000 of an inch and have definite life cycles. They are spread principally by wind blowing the spores.

GIGANTEUM, *with fetching trusses of light crimson and for colder climates. Do not confuse this with the species R. giganteum which will grow to 80 feet.*

IGNATIUS SARGENT, *deep rose flowers will welcome you with their scent. A hardy variety for the background planting.*

Paul E. Genereux

Nematodes measure from 1/50 to 1/25 of an inch long. They move from place to place through the transportation of soil or water. Once in a plant, they move about in the plant's circulative juices.

Other insects move from one plant to another by various means. They may fly, hop or crawl. They may be wafted on air currents, or move by man, animals, and birds. Often careless watering moves them, as it does plant diseases, from one plant to another in the droplets of water.

SOME DO'S AND DON'TS

Here are a few more tips about using sprays and dusts. Avoid inhaling any of these chemicals. Do not allow an inexperienced person to spray or dust your plants. He may harm himself and/or your plants. We are strongly advised by the authorities to spray or dust only when the air is quiet and

VULCAN'S FLAME, *as spectacular as a volcano's erup-
tion. Stands up very well in the hottest of climates.
The plant and flower are much like 'Vulcan', but it
has the advantage of being a single clone rather than
a group variety.*

the foliage is dry. If it is absolutely necessary to spray at other times, the breeze
should be moving away from you and toward
the plants. Wet foliage will cause a dilution
of the spray, reducing its effectiveness.

Always wash your hands and face and
change to clean clothing after this chore.
Wash clothing before wearing it again. Be
careful not to contaminate fish ponds, bird
baths or pet feeding areas. Place toys, lawn
furniture, and other moveable items at a safe

distance. Keep your pets indoors until the
spray has dried or the dust has settled.

Use separate equipment for herbicides and
pesticides or fungicides. It is difficult to
rinse some herbicides from a container and
even a small residue can be disastrous to
your rhododendrons and other plants.

Dispose of empty fertilizer, insecticide and
herbicide containers so that they pose no
hazard to humans, animals or valuable
plants. However, before putting them in the

garbage can, remove the label whether the container is empty or not, and securely attach a sheet of paper which warns that the container held a dangerous poison. Leaving the original label may tempt someone to use the contents without knowing how to do so. Burying old containers is not a wise answer, for they can be dug up later, still containing dangerous residue. Also, as the containers deteriorate, the contents could seep through and pollute land or water. Never attempt to destroy such materials by burning. The aerosol cans will explode, scattering particles of the material. Smoke from the burning chemicals can be as dangerous as the material.

Many of the fungicides and pesticides will keep for several years, if stored properly. The insecticide emulsions break down more rapidly and should be replaced yearly. Salting out or settling of emulsions, balling and lumping of wettable powders and dusts, are signs of breakdown.

Mark the exact date of purchase on a package of insecticide. Never store insecticides or fungicides with weed killers, for the former may absorb some of the herbicide fumes and cause injury to your plants. Chemicals must be kept cool and dry.

MADAME CARVALHO, *soft alluring trusses with greenish spots stop you. Notable for exceptional bud hardiness. Probably a white form of R. catawbiense.*

HARVEST MOON, *the name is well chosen. A spectacular landscape piece which will not outgrow the space allowed.*

THE EQUIPMENT YOU USE IS IMPORTANT

Many gardeners fight the chore of spraying or dusting their plants, and an uphill battle results. Pests and disease which could be avoided by early attention have an opportunity to become well established if treatment is delayed. It is a pretty sound guess that the neglect is caused by lack of proper spraying or dusting apparatus or failure to maintain such equipment in good working order. If your sprayer or duster is an "heirloom" passed from father to son, or if it is in poor condition, remember that the effectiveness of the chemicals will be in proportion to the efficiency of the equipment.

There is a sprayer or duster for every purpose among the many different types and brands offered today. Incidentally, I personally prefer spraying to dusting for the simple reason that rhododendrons are much more handsome with their foliage bright and clean. There is equipment designed for the simple job of treating a few plants or for covering a large garden.

When you visit your favorite garden store to purchase additional rhododendrons, pause for a first hand look at the many different kinds of sprayers and dusters. Check their specifications and capabilities. If you decide to buy, select one that will be easy to handle yet adequate for your needs.

Always keep the sprayer or duster in first-class condition since poorly maintained equipment is inefficient and may damage your plants. Never store a dirty sprayer or duster. Clean them so they will be ready for use immediately when needed. You will save time and money. Remove powder from the dust chamber, rinse and dry it thoroughly. The sprayer should be completely drained of any residue and washed. Force pure water through the hose and nozzle, making certain

KATE WATERER, *heavy trusses bury the foliage with pink color. Quite an effective plant in a garden out of bloom. Will do its best in the shade.*

that no vestige of spray chemical is left to contaminate future chemicals. Clogging of nozzle, hose, and pipe will also be prevented.

Check the sprayer hose frequently and, if it is deteriorating, replace it. Regularly tighten all loose connections and other parts of your sprayer. A blow-off of a hose or nozzle could saturate you with chemical and this might be serious. Replace parts of the spraying apparatus at the first sign of wear. "Safety First" is more important here than in any other phase of gardening.

TRILBY, *a champion red all gardeners love. A dependable grower which possibly is a little more hardy than rated. Can withstand much sun except in more critical climates.*

MOTHER OF PEARL, *not the mother of 'Pink Pearl', as might be suggested, but it is a sport taken from this hybrid. A sport is a single branch with different characteristics brought about by a mutation of cell structure. Like 'Pink Pearl' in every way except for the flowers which open a shell pink and fade to a pure white and have a slight scent.*

COMPLETE COVERAGE

If insect and disease prevention is to be effective, coverage must be thorough with each application of spray or dust. Rhododendrons have huge leaf surfaces but it is easy to see which areas have been covered and which missed. Leaves must be covered beneath and above; branches and trunk too, should be reached.

The spray used to control fungi must completely cover the plant surfaces. A fungicide acts through contact with the leaf surface, preventing germinating spores from mak-

ing contact with the leaf surface. The minute dimensions of fungi spores emphasize the importance of thorough coverage. New systemic fungicides are under test and hopefully will be released soon. Until that time, however, thorough spraying is necessary for prevention of fungus diseases.

Early spring sprays are the most effective against fungus problems, because at that time moisture and temperature are ideal for the germination of fungus spores. Sometimes fall spraying will help in your control program. Choice of fungicides and thoroughness of application are the keys to prevention and control. A series of spraying is required to cover new plant growth, to treat newly germinated fungus spores and to replace the fungicide which has been washed away by rain and irrigation.

Do not spray or dust if there is a threat of rain. A heavy rain will wash away the

COTTON CANDY, *a John Henny rhododendron of appealing beauty. An unusually large spiraling truss with up to 17 florets each four to five inches across. A favorite in the Southeast.*

ROSEUM ELEGANS, *well over a hundred years old.
Without a doubt there are more 'Roseum Elegans'
growing today than any other variety. There are many
forms in cultivation including one called 'Pink Roseum' and another under the name of 'English Roseum'
which is possibly a sport of 'Roseum Elegans'.*

sect problems. Some soil insecticides must be worked into the top six or seven inches of soil for any degree of effectiveness. For this reason, these insecticides are difficult to use around rhododendrons which have many, many roots close to the soil surface.

THE DISEASES

I have no intention of discouraging you from using rhodies because they occasionally are bothered by certain fungus diseases. These diseases usually are not difficult to prevent. Use one of the ferbam materials, giving the plants a thorough spraying just after flowering as the new foliage starts to appear. Repeat the spraying two or three times at ten day intervals. Follow the manufacturer's directions, and be sure the spray contains a good spreader-sticker.

There are several kinds of leaf spots caused by fungi. It is difficult for the gardener to identify them but, fortunately, the

chemicals before they have a chance to do their work. Many materials require hours, or longer, to be effective. I do not recommend the heat of the day for spraying. Morning or early evening is preferable, provided the spray has time to dry before nightfall. Morning dew could dilute a liquid spray; slight moisture will aid adhesion of a dust spray.

Insects breathe through their body covering, and even a droplet of oil will prevent breathing and kill them. The problem is to apply that film of oil, or oil chemical, so that it covers their bodies.

Whether an insect causes damage to your plants by chewing or sucking is not important nowadays, because modern insecticides have a lap-over control. Use the general types of insecticides I recommend earlier in this chapter for better control of specific in-

CORNUBIA, *the handsome foliage provides a suitable
setting for the ball-of-red truss. The waxen flowers
are beautiful in a woodsy landscape. A trip through
Northern California in February when 'Cornubia' is
aflame in gardens is magnificent.*

Henry R. Yates

MARY BELLE, *one of Joe Gable's newest and best productions. It will be hard to find for a few years. The flowers have heavy substance.*

ferbam type fungicides are effective for prevention and control. Remember that leaf spotting often is caused by other conditions, such as mechanical injury, poor soil and drainage, drought, improper fertilizing, freeze damage, winter sun scald and sun scorch in summer. When you are certain that weather and culture are not causing the leaf spots, start your spray program.

A few other fungus diseases sometimes attack rhododendrons. Branch blight, gray mold (Botrytis), wilt, rusts, certain galls and root rot can occur but are not common. If you contact your county agent or state agricultural college, they will give you expert advice about the newest methods of prevention and control.

SAPPHO, *the large, spectacular truss of contrast seems to be preferred more frequently by the male sex. Sometimes rejected due to legginess which requires extra effort to control. An informal woodland setting would be natural and a solution to the problem.*

Clifford A. Fenner

MARCHIONESS OF LANSDOWNE, *a proud beauty with arresting contrasts. A dependable bloomer on a plant which will show color up to six weeks. Quite hardy as well as heat tolerant.*

PARASITIC PLANTS

Midway between the fungus and pest problems is another which occurs in some parts of the country from the parasitic plant, Cuscuta. This noxious plant attaches itself to rhododendrons by absorption organs which will suck the moisture from the rhodies. Fortunately, it is easy to spot because of the orange-yellow runners which occur in early summer. Pull it out before it has a chance to produce seed.

INSECTS

The damage to rhododendrons caused by insect pests sometimes is more obvious, and the "culprits" can be more readily identified, than fungus diseases. However, if one of the general-purpose insecticides mentioned earlier does not give good control, get help from the experts.

Rhododendron lace bugs are flat insects about one-eighth inch long. Lacy wings cover their bodies in the adult stage. Nymphs, which result from eggs laid on the under surface of leaves along the midribs, and the adults suck plant juices. This causes a mottled or speckled appearance on the upper surface of the leaves. Severe infestation can cause a coalescence of individual feeding spots into a grayish-green discoloration that may eventually turn brown. Almost any good contact spray containing nicotine, pyrethrum, rotenone, lindane, chlordane, or malathion will control them.

Aphids do occur on rhododendrons, usually attacking the young leaves in the spring, but they are not much of a threat. A severe infestation can cause some curling and twisting of leaves, so it is advisable to keep aphids off your plants. Use diazinon, malathion or lindane sprays for quick control.

White flies are irritating to the gardener as they fly about him, and damage rhododendrons by sucking plant juice from the undersides of the leaves. They are easily identified by their creamy white color and small size (about one-tenth inch). Use a contact spray to control them.

Different species of spider mites attack rhododendrons, as well as most other garden shrubs. Minute in size, they feed on both the upper and lower surfaces of the leaves. We are seldom troubled with them here in our moist Pacific Northwest climate, but they can be a more serious problem where summers are hot and dry. If not controlled, they can cause considerable damage to the plants. And in the home greenhouse, they can become a serious threat because they multiply so rapidly there. Indoors, you will probably have to use a good miticide, but outdoors I suggest using malathion for their control.

HENRIETTA SARGENT, *well-spaced trusses show off to good advantage. Note the ground cover of ivy. Although the flower is similar to 'Mrs. Charles S. Sargent', it is a more compact and slower grower.*

Don Gray

108

Don Gray

four ounces of chlordane dust to each 1,000 square feet, working it into the soil or mulch gently to avoid damage to the roots. Follow the manufacturer's directions.

The obscure root weevil is usually brownish-gray in color. The adults can riddle the leaves of rhododendrons, notching the leaves heavily. White legless larvae live in the soil. Malathion, dust or spray, and diazinon spray are good control materials. Foliage, soil and any adjacent debris should be treated about June 1, repeating the treatment in July and a third time in August if the infestation is severe. Use of a soil insecticide at the time of planting is effective.

Thrips, too, can attack rhododendrons, as well as many other kinds of garden plants. The tiny thrips cause a blotched appearance on the upper surface of leaves and a silvery substance on the under surface. Lindane,

WHEATLEY, *the border is better with this one. Among the best from the Dexter collection of some wonderful seedlings. A good quality plant. Will stand some sun.*

Don Gray

The spray or dust should cover the foliage thoroughly both beneath and above.

Black vine weevils have a black snout and are from one-fourth to three-eighths of an inch long. They are wingless, move slowly and avoid strong light. They emerge in late May and throughout June, and will feed lightly on rhododendron foliage, chewing out small holes generally near the margin of the leaves. Sometimes they feed on the bark of large roots, the crowns, or stems of plants. The adults should be killed before they lay their eggs. Insecticides such as chlordane, heptachlor and dieldrin will kill the adults, eggs and young larvae that are near the surface of the soil. Spray the foliage, and especially the soil around the plant, using about one pint of spray to each square foot of soil beneath the branches. Or you can use

malathion, nicotine, pyrethrum or rotenone sprays are recommended for thrip control. Lindane and malathion have a good residual action.

Various caterpillars or beetles may chew on your rhododendron foliage from time to time, but the harm they do usually is negligible. Regular treatment with a good spray such as methoxychlor in late June and again in July should keep these pests away. Follow the manufacturer's dilution recommendation.

The rhododendron borer is the larva of a moth closely related to the peach tree borer. Eggs are laid on the new growth, the main stem or on large limbs of rhododendrons by the moths in late May or early June. The larvae then bore into the plants. Remove and destroy badly damaged plant parts. If the infestation is minor, you can destroy the insect by probing the holes with a wire or flexible twig or by cutting them out with a knife.

R. SMIRNOWII, *a rugged species which will stand much exposure. The thick woolly indumentum under the leaves is particularly attractive on the new growth. A densely foliaged plant which usually spreads much more than its height.*

TONY, *possibly one of Tony Shammarello's most popular hybrids. Excellent performer in cold and hot climates.*

Otherwise, spray the plants about the time the adults emerge and start laying eggs, from mid-June to the first of July. This will kill the adults, but not the borers already in the plants. Preventing reproduction will control or eliminate this pest.

Scales, I believe, are rather easily recognized by most gardeners. Both the rhododendron and the oleander scale sometimes attack rhododendrons. Feeding by scales will cause yellowish and, later on, reddish spots on rhododendron leaves. When both the leaves and stems are heavily infested, the plant becomes noticeably more unhealthy month by month. If not checked, the plants can be killed. The use of DDT to control scale insects apparently has demonstrated one of its many unexpected, serious side effects. DDT, used over a period of time, seems to kill off the natural predators that keep scales under control. A gardener's safest method of control is to spray with a miscible oil of two per cent strength. Completely cover all parts

MEDUSA, *with richest bells of orange. Quite similar to 'Fabia' except that the plant is a little denser, the foliage has a lighter indumentum, and the blooms have more orange coloring. Does very well in Alabama.*

BELLE HELLER, *golden splotching is like spattering from flipped paint brush. Largest flowers and purest color of the hardy whites with yellow blotch.*

of the plants when they are in their dormant period in late winter, or early in spring just before new growth starts. It is important to choose a time when the spray will have an opportunity to dry. If the temperature is below 45 degrees Fahrenheit or is apt to fall below that temperature before drying is complete, delay spraying. Summer sprays can be used in June during the scales' half-grown stage. At that time, use a malathion spray with sticker-spreader, properly diluted, applying it in mid-June and again in early July. This will kill the insects before they mature.

If you note sharp crescent holes in rhododendron foliage, they could be caused by the beetles of the cranberry rootworm, a brown or chestnut-colored oval beetle. A good insecticide applied from mid-June to early August should eliminate them.

The rhododendron midge sometimes feeds on the under-surface of rhododendron leaves. It causes the margins of small leaves to roll under and fold over the midrib, and the leaves become pale greenish-yellow. Progression of the problem causes brownish spotting. Adults of this pest are small, yellowish, frail flies only one-twentieth of an inch long. Larvae cause injury in late May and early June, and the damage continues on secondary growth in July and August. They often cause severe damage on greenhouse plants. The proper insecticide should be applied every ten days to two weeks, when the plants are growing rapidly. It kills the adult flies, but the young maggots mostly survive. This, again, is a case of preventing reproduction in order to control a pest.

Injury sometimes occurs to rhododendrons from the giant hornet. The adult chews the bark to make material for building its nest. This hornet is an inch or more long, and has an overall yellow-brown coloring with black markings. It often builds its nest in the ground near rhododendrons, lilacs and weigela. Spray or dust the nests with one of the newer insecticides I suggested earlier.

The pitted ambrosia beetle occasionally attacks old rhododendron plants. This small dark-brown beetle tunnels into the main stems just above ground level. After the stems have become honeycombed, they readily break off. The best control is to remove the affected smaller stems or the whole plant, if badly infected. Another control measure is wrapping the infected trunk areas with burlap that has been soaked in a recommended insecticide. The beetles will be destroyed as they emerge from their tunnels.

RODENTS

Mice are a serious problem in some parts of the United States. Their abundance varies from year to year and apparently follows a

MRS. C. B. VAN NES, *you will thrill with its rosy red buds, and the nearly red opening flowers which soon turn to glowing pink. Does not branch well with pruning.*

Azaleas always meld gracefully with rhododendrons, and the addition of a woodland environment lends even more fascinating harmony to the setting. An enchanting scene photographed in Canada.

cyclic pattern. They attack rhododendron and other plant roots and stems during the winter when food is scarce, and they can kill or badly injure the plants. Make every effort to keep mice and other rodents under tight control at all times. They often cause damage when snow is on the ground and you are not aware of the problem. The best answer is to eliminate the mice, rats, moles and gophers by trapping and by using poison baits during the warm seasons when their control is easiest. Eliminate hiding and nesting places when possible, and spread bait before winter mulching your rhodies. Moles, while mostly interested in earthworms and grubs, will eat a certain amount of vegeta-

tive growth, principally the roots of plants. Follow the best procedures for your area as recommended by specialists in rodent control.

NUTRIENT DEFICIENCIES

You will find it helpful to learn the natural shade of green of the particular rhododendron varieties you already have or wish to buy. The varieties normally vary considerably in color, from a rather light green to one that is quite dark. By knowing the normal green shading, you will be able to recognize a plant that is suffering from nitrogen deficiency. A gardener who properly prepares and maintains his soil rarely has a deficiency problem. Lighter colored foliage than is normal for a particular variety,

MRS. BETTY ROBERTSON, *as frilly and rich as a lady's formal. Notice the peculiar twist in the dark foliage. A slow grower which is best in slight shade.*

stunted growth, stalks too slender and few new side shoots indicate a nitrogen deficiency. The lower leaves often are a lighter green than the upper ones, or may be yellow. Sometimes the deficiency shows only in the lower, older leaves. Yellowing is followed by their drying to a light brown color. Normal shedding of the old leaves occurs slowly.

If a phosphorus deficiency exists, the foliage is darker than normal and shoot growth is retarded. Sometimes there is a yellowing between the veins on the lower leaves. Generally the leaf coloring is purplish, especially on the stalks. The symptoms may be localized on the lower leaves.

A potassium deficiency also is usually localized in the older, lower leaves. Dead leaf margins and tips occur and the leaves appear mottled. Yellowing begins at the leaf margins and moves toward the center. Finally, the margins curl under and turn brown. Older leaves usually drop.

Magnesium deficiency or magnesium chlorosis produces a light-colored, nearly yellow foliage. This yellowish-ivory color lies between the veins, although the veins and adjacent tissues remain green. Dolomitic lime can be used to correct this deficiency, if the soil is very acid. For other, more normal soils, I recommend magnesium sulfate (Epsom salts) at the rate of one-half pound per 100 square feet. Some careful experimenting may be necessary before you try to correct a magnesium deficiency, because varieties respond differently.

PIONEER, *the profuse blooming appearance results from flowers in each leaf axil along the stem. Responds well to heavy pruning. Referred to as semi-deciduous because all leaves are replaced each spring. Excellent in mass plantings as this highway landscape. Blooms with Forsythia.*

P.J.M., *glossy-green foliage of summer becomes mahogany-colored in winter. The initials are those of the producer, P. J. Mezitt. Reported to bloom beautifully after exposure in temperature of 30 degrees below zero. An excellent landscape plant as it will grow under almost any conditions and the flowers are long-lasting.*

Correcting deficiences of any of the three major elements is rather simple, if you use a fertilizer designed for that particular purpose. If all three nutrients are deficient, the answer, of course, is a balanced fertilizer.

Fertilizers are available which contain not only the three major elements, but also the minor elements, such as iron, copper and zinc. Unless you have an unusual soil problem, you can purchase a ready-mixed fertilizer containing the needed trace elements. Iron is the minor element most likely to be deficient. The symptoms are green leaves with chlorotic areas between the veins. If the problem becomes acute, the leaf tips and margins will die and turn brown.

MECHANICAL DAMAGE

I am certain that anyone rough-handling a rhododendron does not realize how easily the stems and leaves can be injured. The sturdy look of this lovely shrub is somewhat misleading. Avoid windy places in the landscape. Rhododendrons have large leaves, for the most part, and these are easily whipped around and broken. Leaf petioles can be cracked and the leaves will then dangle from

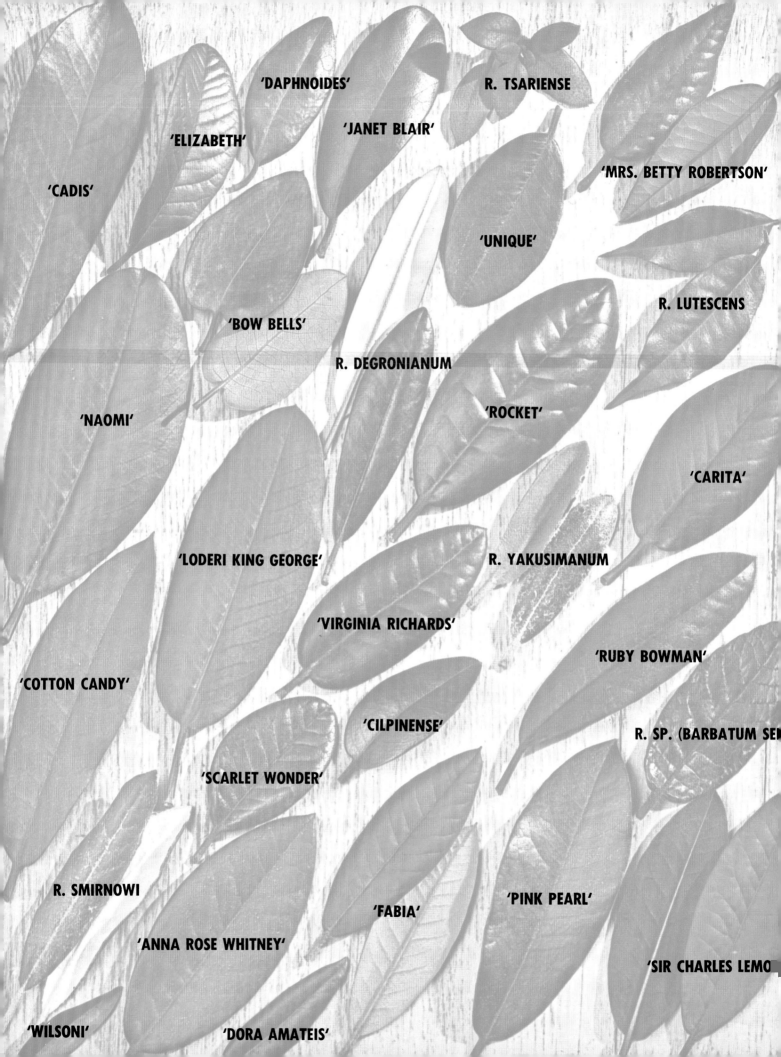

the branches, or the leaves can be snapped off completely.

The banging of rhodie leaves against one another and against other plants can damage them. In addition to the ragged appearance of the leaves, such damage is an invitation to fungus diseases. If unavoidable damage occurs, remove the broken branches and leaves. Treat large wounds with any standard sealing compound available at garden centers.

Another physiological problem which kills many woody plants, including rhododendrons, is girdling. In less severe cases, gir-

LODERI KING GEORGE, *ten or more deliciously scented flowers up to seven inches across in each truss. Allow plenty of room, and provide wind and sun protection.*

Leo F. Simon

HURRICANE, *pinks have a singularly happy effect in the garden. Similar to 'Mrs. Furnival' but with larger flowers and foliage, and more perfect plant habit.*

dling may cause slow, unhealthy, misshapen growth. When the inner bark around the trunk base of a rhododendron is destroyed, the entire plant will die. If the bark is only partially damaged, the plant may eventually overcome the problem by gradually replacing the lost vital tissue. Food manufactured by the leaves is routed to the root system through the bark tissues. When girdling occurs, the plant slowly starves.

Girdling, in its earliest stages, may be mistaken for nitrogen deficiency because the foliage turns pale. Next the leaves droop and curl, eventually turning brown and dropping. By then, the plant is probably already dying or dead. Prevention of girdling is the answer.

Remove any labels which are tightly wired around the trunk or branches. As the plant grows, the wires tighten and, in time, girdling will take place. Use a paper type label or a plastic stake-type in the ground, or you can loop a wire label loosely around a small branch. Wire girdling usually damages only a portion of a plant. Prune out the dead part, and then reshape the plant over several seasons by careful pruning.

Insects and plant diseases, too, may cause girdling of rhododendrons and other plants in your garden. Mice and other rodents and the careless use of garden tools are sometimes involved in girdling. Prevention of the problem is much more effective than treating the damage later.

More subtle, but nonetheless just as deadly, is girdling caused by a fall or spring freeze which may kill the bark area two or three inches above the soil surface. The

PURPLE LACE, *did Belgium ever produce finer lace than this? Too new for full evaluation, but it appears to have some advantages over 'Purple Splendour'.*

PRAECOX *and* R. MUCRONULATUM, *the wonderful lilac color contrasts beautifully with yellow tulips in the spring. 'Praecox' seems to sense impending early frosts and will not usually flower if grown in the open. This variety can be readily sheared to make an attractively low hedge. 'Mucronulatum' is an unusual deciduous variety of extreme hardiness which flowers freely.*

trunk at this point is very susceptible to a sudden freeze, which cracks the bark, exposing the woody inner cylinder. If the dead bark completely encircles the trunk, loss of the plant is almost certain. Do not destroy it immediately, however. There is a chance that enough of the cambium tissue may have survived to regenerate a sound layer of bark and save the plant.

Give a girdled plant extra attention, especially water, to help it survive. Apply a wound sealing compound to the damaged area and wrap it securely with burlap. Prevention of freeze damage includes wrapping the lower part of choice specimens and the less hardy rhododendrons with layers of protective burlap in the fall. You can also heap sawdust or other mulch material around the trunks of the plants to a depth of several inches. Remove these protections as soon as the danger of severe frosts has passed. Leaving them may cause other problems.

CHAPTER NINE

Rhododendrons In The Greenhouse

 Those of you who are interested in forcing rhododendrons into flower may find this chapter and the next helpful. Today's best method of bringing rhododendrons into flower out of season is tied in with the use of growth regulants. Temperature and "long day" (added light beyond that of normal daylight) are associated with growth regulants, so I am including much about greenhouse culture in the chapter covering growth retardants and their use.

Probably most of the rhododendrons would respond well to greenhouse forcing, but I think you would be wise to select a few varieties which seem to show the best tendencies or which have been recommended for forcing. However, as you learn to limit growth of those varieties which normally grow quite large before flowering, I believe you will discover a whole new dimension of interest and enjoyment in growing many rhododendrons for winter color in the greenhouse or in your home.

Rhododendrons, with their breath-taking beauty of bloom and their elegant foliage, make splendid potted plants when forced. I predict that the time is not far away when people who want the best in potted plants will force rhododendrons in their own home greenhouses, or purchase them from florists and garden shops, who will be marketing more of these quality plants produced by commercial greenhouse growers.

It was my good fortune to donate some of the rhododendron plants to Dr. Richard A. Criley, now an assistant professor of horticulture at the University of Hawaii, which he used in his graduate research work on forcing rhododendrons and using growth regulants. Among the varieties studied, he concluded that 'Anah Kruschke' and 'Marinus Koster' respond well to the forcing-regulant treatment. The flower form and size of 'Anah Kruschke', in particular, were excellent. In the next chapter, I mention that growth regulants do not have a uniform effect on all varieties, and he found this to be true with 'Beauty of Littleworth', which did not respond well at all.

Others who have done important research work with Van Veen rhododendrons are Dr. H. M. Cathey, Head of Ornamentals Investigations, USDA, Beltsville, Maryland, and Prof. D. C. Kiplinger, of Ohio State University, Columbus, Ohio.

I am sure you will want to consider another factor as you experiment with forcing rhododendrons in your home greenhouse. While most varieties will produce flowers, they may lose something in the process. In other words, a rhododendron which produces fine quality flowers and trusses outdoors may not necessarily do so when forced. Criley found this to be true to some extent with

'Marinus Koster'. The shape of the forced flower truss was not as good as the natural bloom grown outdoors.

My good friend and rhododendron expert, J. Harold Clarke, Ph.D., and various other rhododendron producers, list in their catalogs a number of varieties recommended for forcing. I see every indication that current lists of forcing varieties will grow in the next few years. Commercial greenhouse operators are already taking a long hard look at the idea, and they undoubtedly will be experimenting with many different varieties. I see no reason why you should not join the fun and do some private experimentation yourself. Why not try some of the tender species, such as those from the Malay peninsula and other warm areas?

As I mentioned earlier, the best flowering response comes from rhododendrons which have received ample phosphorus. Criley found this to be true in his experiments.

There are two important factors involved with forcing rhododendrons:

GENERAL EISENHOWER, *worthy of its famous name. Sunlight through the ruffled edges further amplifies the beauty of these large, rich-red flowers. The plant habit is quite similar to 'Britannia'.*

(1) A storage period of eight to ten weeks at 45 to 50 degrees Fahrenheit is required to induce a dormancy period in the plants which are to be forced. A plant taken into the greenhouse for forcing without this "substitute for winter" will not respond to subsequent treatment. During cold storage, about ten foot-candles of light are needed for twelve hours daily. I cannot emphasize strongly enough the importance of maintaining proper moisture. Keep in mind that plants in storage are not in a period of active growth and do not require the normal amount of water. At the same time, dehydration can quickly damage or destroy plants in storage.

(2) It is very important, when forcing rhododendrons, to supply light for four hours during the middle of the night. Dr. Criley used this period of light in his experiments, but I believe it will be found that specific varieties require different light pe-

R. AUGUSTINII, *truly a heavenly blue for one discriminating in colors. There are many forms of this species which vary in shades of blue and hardiness. It is interesting that the more tender forms are the best blues.*

SAFFRON QUEEN, *a greenhouse variety except for warm climates. The color holds well in partial shade which the plant needs. Can be grown as an espalier and it will tolerate extensive shearing for more compact growth.*

riods at night. In the next chapter, I discuss more thoroughly forcing temperatures and the light factor, both the application and the total time requirement.

Let me stress the importance of good ventilation when forcing rhododendrons. Keep in mind that they are plants which originated in a cold climate, and that moving them into a greenhouse does not change this basic preference. Those of you who live in warmer climates will find it best to force rhododendrons when outside temperatures are cool. If you have a thoroughly modern greenhouse, complete with an air cooling system, you can induce the plants to break dormancy through the combination of cold storage and the effect of the greenhouse cooling system after you start forcing them.

HOLDEN, *certainly worthy of your landscape. One of the finest of the Shammarello hybrids. Does well in both cold and warm climates. The flower buds are exceptionally large.*

Maintain light moisture conditions at all times. When the sun is bright, regardless of the time of year, plants in the greenhouse can dry out much faster than you may think possible. Rhododendrons suffering from drought will likely not force properly, no matter how well they are watered thereafter. Open up your greenhouse for a short time each day. A complete change of air is helpful in achieving successful forcing.

GREENHOUSE PESTS

Chapter VIII does a thorough job of telling you how to prevent pest and disease problems on your rhododendrons in the landscape. I will mention two particular insects which may give you more trouble in the greenhouse than outdoors, so that you will be prepared to prevent them. They are thrips and cyclamen mites.

To prevent mites from getting a foothold, use a good miticide recommended by your garden center. Once entrenched, mites stop or distort the growth of your greenhouse rhododendrons. They also cause flowers to be poorly colored and misshapen. Prevention during the earliest stages of infestation is necessary, because mites work on the tender plant tips and buds. Once established, they are almost impossible to eliminate from your rhodie plants.

Thrips will greatly reduce a plant's vitality, consuming juices and disfiguring the leaf surface. They will also damage buds and

WILGEN'S RUBY, *could hold its own with gems in a jeweler's window. A newer hybrid of good form which shows much promise.*

LATH HOUSES

Your joy of gardening with rhododendrons can be extended with a lath house or other permanent shade structure, where you can place some of your favorite varieties in beds or in containers. The houses can range from ones made of rough boards in conventional lath-house fashion to rather elaborate and interesting designs for additional beauty in your landscape. A simple one can be made using shading material of plastic screen (Saran cloth). As I mentioned earlier, it comes in a soft shade of green, complementary to your plants inside and outside. It can be purchased with varying degrees of shade potential, meeting the need in your particular area. The shade structure makes possible the growing of certain varieties that otherwise could not even be considered.

flowers and spoil their appearance. Malathion and lindane are favored control sprays for thrips in the greenhouse. You probably have noted that I have not recommended DDT for outdoor or indoor use. The use of this chemical has already caused alarming and perhaps irreversible damage to man's total environment. There are other means of preventing and controlling the undesirable insects without using this chemical.

When rhododendrons are used indoors, give a little extra attention to their placement in your home. Each plant should have the best light situation possible, even though you may have to provide supplemental light from an artificial source. A cool spot will lengthen the time you will be able to enjoy the plant. To provide a little extra humidity, place the container on pebbles in a saucer or tray, keeping the water level just at the top of the pebbles. And do check the moisture frequently. The dry atmosphere of the average home quickly removes it.

GOLDSWORTH YELLOW, *most hardy of the older yellow rhododendrons. Although this is cream colored, the yellowness is accentuated by the buds opening a shade of apricot pink. It is best observed in subdued light. 'Goldsworth Yellow' is not too prevalent because of the difficulty of rooting it from cuttings.*

BLUE ENSIGN, *a later blooming 'Blue Peter' with better plant habit and stronger foliage. 'Odee Wright' is in the background.*

Whereas the moisture requirements of rhododendrons are increased in a greenhouse, the opposite is true in a shade house. Less air circulates through the lath house than in the garden, and the temperature is reduced considerably. This means there is less transpiration from the plants. Except for a shade house with a high roof, you may have to alter your thinking a bit regarding installation of a sprinkling system, putting it on the outside of the roof rather than inside. A low structure will not permit good distribution of water, but sprinklers overhead on the outside will work satisfactorily.

One more point in favor of a shade house for your choice rhododendrons is about five degrees more frost protection. Probably you can extend the range of varieties you grow and be less apt to lose any of them during unusual weather extremes.

CHAPTER TEN

Growth Regulators

Just as we get our minds comfortably settled, thinking that the ultimate in growing methods and materials has been reached, along comes someone who says "tain't so," and thus it will always be. This is one reason plants are so intriguing in the landscape or indoors in a greenhouse or home. New growing techniques and materials will be

developed to stretch the limits of the imagination, even in this "space age."

The latest "miracle" has to do with the use of growth regulators. I think that, used on rhododendrons, the greatest advantage now and for some time in the future is in the greenhouse rather than outdoors. Later I explain the reason for this belief. In this space age, who is so bold to say that the day will not come when we can grow rhododen-

GOLDFORT, *a fine light yellow of good habit, but I can find no gold in it. The beautiful foliage inherited from R. fortunei makes it better than 'Goldsworth Yellow', but it is not quite as hardy.*

LAMPLIGHTER, *worthy enough to light up any garden. Quite similar to 'Britannia' with the advantage of easier propagation from cuttings. The blooms have a wonderful glow when the sun is behind the flower.*

drons and all other plants to our specific needs, designed to fit any situation, large or small? Certainly not I. For quite some time I have been of the opinion that new horticultural vistas are opening, and we have had only a peek at things to come. So hold on to your hat and be ready to expand your thinking as you continue to garden.

Although the Japanese seemed to have considerable knowledge about the gibberellins, it was not until 1956 that we began to hear American plant scientists were discovering some amazing effects of gibberellic acid on plant growth. We learned then that this material, an acid extracted from a fungus grown in a liquid culture medium, could

cause bush beans to produce twining vines and grow as pole beans; produce dwarf-size peas on plants taller than normal tall-types; stimulate stocks so that the linear growth is better and faster; mature certain other flowers faster than normal; and generally cause many other unexpected growth changes.

Scientists and chemists began to consider these astonishing effects. If this chemical, gibberellic acid, could affect plant growth, was it not entirely possible that other chemicals, natural or synthetic, could also induce radical changes in growth? Perhaps their studies would result in new chemicals and application techniques. In time, along came the various Phosfons, Cycocel and B-Nine, to name the most prominent, all beneficial to commercial and amateur growers.

Soon some enterprising person began wondering about the effects of growth retardants on rhododendrons. Most of the many beautiful rhododendron varieties naturally grow very slowly, and only start to produce flowers in their second and third year. Now it has been proved that a growth retardant correctly used, greatly reduces the time needed to grow and to force flowering of rhododendrons in a greenhouse. Plants which are a manageable size for use inside the home can be produced. I predict there is a great opportunity for commercial growers who specialize in forcing plants for the florist trade. What other shrub can match the elegance and beauty of a rhododendron in full bloom!

For reasons yet unknown, the retardants do not work consistently. The response of different varieties varies considerably. If you should try the idea in your greenhouse, first get information about which varieties re-

BROUGHTONII AUREUM, *as rich as the more expensive spread. An extremely interesting Azaleodendron with a sweet scent. Heavy pruning will make a better plant. Blooms with 'Purple Splendour'.*

Rhododendrons can be grown in most any part of the Americas, but proper variety selection is important. Major rhododendron growers are knowledgeable and are most willing to offer assistance. Michigan City, Indiana is the location of these garden scenes.

Don Urquhart

ROSAMUNDI, *flowers for March enjoyment. Sometimes confused with 'Christmas Cheer' which is an earlier bloomer and lower grower with smaller foliage and trusses of a lighter pink color.*

R. STRIGILLOSUM, *like a grove of palm trees. This species is included to show the possibilities for unique landscape situations. Blood red flowers will add to the charm.*

ELISABETH HOBBIE, *wonderful low growth combined with huge handsome foliage. This is one of a series of new hybrids just becoming available in this country. The breeder is Dietrich Hobbie of Germany. It is a splendid year-around hybrid for the rockery or low border. It is quite hardy as well as heat tolerant.*

spond best to forcing. Then obtain plants in the size recommended for best results with the use of a growth regulant.

Be certain to follow directions to the last detail. Even then, I would experiment on a few plants. One usually needs to "get the feel of" a new procedure, mainly because each gardener has his own way of handling plants and the environment of his greenhouse is different from any other. It is not as dangerous, however, to give a plant a moderate overdose of a growth regulant, as it is to overfeed the plant. The growth retardants are temperamental, too, in the way they act at different seasons of the year. Some perform better in winter months while others give best results in the summer.

The process is still considered experimental, but here are some suggestions regarding the use of B-Nine on rhododendrons in the greenhouse. Basically, the requirement is to to 2 a.m. The new vegetative growth of the plant is slowed by the retardant. To control the additional two or three flushes of growth, characteristic of rhododendrons before bud initiation, two more applications of retardant are required at 30 day intervals. Follow the manufacturer's directions explicitly regarding the amounts of retardant and fertilizer and methods of application.

The plant should be transferred to natural day-length conditions after two months, if treatment is in the summer, or after four months if treated in the winter. In either case, flower buds should be visible within about four months. Two more months of natural daylight should cause full development of the flower buds. Up to this point temperature control is not mandatory. Thereafter, a temperature of 55 degrees Fahrenheit should be maintained, along with

BEAUTY OF LITTLEWORTH, *a brick wall provides perfect frame for a picture of white beauty. Shy to show her buds in youth, with maturity she is much more bold with huge trusses that are long-lasting. Good vigor and habit makes a perfect screen plant.*

spray with B-Nine once a month for three months and to provide "long days." Remember that indicated time periods are approximations and that there is a difference in varietal response.

Start with a liner (rooted cutting that is established). Plant in a mixture of peat moss and perlite. If you use a container, be certain it is designed to give adequate drainage. Treat the plant at once with the growth retardant and maintain "long days" with 20 foot-candles of artificial light from 10 p.m.

BESSE HOWELLS, *flowers like crinkled Christmas paper. A dependable, heavy bud set every year.*

JINGLE BELLS, *buds, flowers and foliage attract attention. A fascinating new semi-dwarf.*

continuous light equivalent to 10 foot-candles of incandescent light, for an approximate period of two and one-half months, depending upon response of the variety. Then increase the temperature to 65 degrees, with continuous 10 foot-candles of light, for about one and one-half to two and one-half months to force the plant into flower.

CHAPTER ELEVEN

The Species And The Hybrids

The future use of rhododendrons in the landscape presents two images, both beautiful. Because so many superb new hybrids have joined those developed during past decades, emphasis has been quite heavy on these lovely plants with their wide array of unusual colors, habit and foliage. A definite interest in species has evolved recently, however, and a demand for them will increase in the years ahead.

It is quite natural that gardeners, amateur and expert, would find their whetted curiosity ranging beyond the use of hybrids, as they appease their desire for all the new varieties. The logical step, then, is to seek the wonders nature wrought as she adapted rhododendrons for many different areas of the world.

The nearly 1000 species of this magnificent genus run the course of plant size from a bare two inches in height to trees reaching 80 feet into the air. And, their range of form, foliage and flowers is equally impressive. Almost any gardener will find many of the rhododendron species interesting and important for his landscape.

It has been a most difficult task to prepare this list of species, because almost all varieties have their own special appeal. This selection is representative of the wide variation of plant forms among the rhododendron species, and would make an excellent collection. If desire and space reach beyond my recommendations, a great many more of the species are worthy of growing. Although the propagation of species to date has been limited to certain varieties, continue your search, for I am certain the list of available species will increase greatly in the years ahead.

The temperature shown in each case is the minimum which the variety will stand under normal gardening procedures. With added protection, it is generally possible for it to withstand a few degrees lower temperature. The indicated time of blooming is the month the variety usually is in flower in the Northwest. You will find a picture of the variety where a page number is indicated.

| *R. aberconwayi* | MAY | 0° |
| Irroratum series | White, pink | Medium |

Long, recurved leaves of leathery substance. Slight flush of pink in a saucer-shaped flower with dark spotting on the upper lobe.

| *R. augustinii* | APRIL | +5° |
| Triflorum series | Blue | Tall |

Bushy shrub with pointed soft green leaves. Many selected forms available in various shades of blue. Seedlings are not reliable in color. Page 123.

R. bureavii	MAY	0°
Taliense series	Rose	Tall

A magnificent foliage plant with a brilliant hairy coating. Slow to flower but it will then bloom freely.

R. calophytum	MARCH	−5°
Fortunei series	White, pink	Tall

Large-leaved, small tree variety, which must be protected from wind. Fragrant flowers in a large truss of white to pink with a bright red blotch and a conspicuous yellow stigma.

R. campylogynum	MAY	0°
Campylogynum series	Pink, purple, crimson	Semi-dwarf

Small-leaved variety, excellent for the rock garden in the smaller forms. Flowers are little nodding bells available in a wide range of colors. Page 78.

R. carolinianum	MAY	−25°
Carolinianum series	Pink to rose	Medium

A native American species with a neat, attractive growth habit. The small leaves are glossy green with the undersides presenting a rusty appearance. It will easily produce an abundance of small flowers.

R. fastigiatum	APRIL	−10°
Lapponicum series	Blue, purple	Dwarf

A densely foliaged plant which will fit well in the rockery. The small flower clusters completely cover this alpine plant.

R. fictolacteum	APRIL	−5°
Falconeri series	White, rose	Tall

A large-leaved tree rhododendron grown primarily for its foliage which is attractive in the cinnamon-brown furry coating of the new shoots, and the orange, felty indumentum under the older shining, dark-green leaves. The bell-shaped flowers in large trusses appear with a deep red blotch.

R. forrestii var. *repens*	APRIL	+5°
Neriiflorum series	Red	Dwarf

A creeping, alpine with small leaves. Tubular, bright red flowers in strikingly large size. Must have perfect drainage.

R. fortunei	MAY	−15°
Fortunei series	White, pink	Tall

A large-leaved plant, free from pests, and most attractive. Large clusters of flowers are exceptionally fragrant.

R. impeditum	APRIL	−10°
Lapponicum series	Blue	Dwarf

A dense growing, tiny-leaved, rounded mound of a plant which should be grown in the sun for maximum compactness. One of the best, small, blue-flowered species suitable for rock gardens, edging for beds, or as a border plant. Page 92.

R. keiskei	APRIL	−5°
Triflorum series	Lemon-yellow	Low

The dwarf form is recommended as it is a more compact and attractive plant with olive-green leaves. It blooms profusely with clusters of bell-shaped flowers. Page 75.

R. keleticum	JUNE	−10°
Saluenense series	Purple-crimson	Dwarf

A handsome, dense, matted shrublet with aromatic leaves. The flowers, with crimson flecks, are large in proportion to the plant. May be used effectively as a Bonsai plant.

| *R. lutescens* | APRIL | 0° |
| Triflorum series | Yellow | Tall |

Distinctive for the bronzy red foliage of the new growth. The long narrow leaves later turn to dark green. A heavy bloomer with light green spots on the upper petal.

| *R. makinoi* | JUNE | −10° |
| Ponticum series | White, rose, scarlet | Low |

Extremely long, narrow leaves, heavily indumented with a greyish felty covering. The new shoots are coated with a silvery down. Mounded, tight trusses with good pure color.

| *R. minus* | JUNE | −25° |
| Carolinianum series | Lavender-rose, pink, white | Tall |

Extremely tolerant of heat and cold, this plant in its better forms can be used as a fine background in larger gardens. The funnel-shaped flowers appear in late June, in large rounded trusses with as many as 30 florets.

| *R. moupinense* | MARCH | 0° |
| Moupinense series | White, rose | Semi-dwarf |

A fine plant for a container or Bonsai effects. Needs protection from early frosts. Large, funnel-shaped, fragrant flowers with red spots.

| *R. mucronulatum* | FEBRUARY | −25° |
| Dauricum series | Rose-purple to pink | Medium |

This is a deciduous rhododendron which is often confused with an azalea. Striking because of early flowering which frosts might damage, but there are always more unopened buds ready for the next bit of warm weather. 'Cornell Pink' is a named form of pleasing color. Heavy shearing will result in compactness and greater blooming. Page 120.

| *R. pemakoense* | APRIL | 0° |
| Uniflorum series | Lilac-pink | Low |

One of the best of the dwarfs. The flowering is so free that often it is difficult to see the foliage. Massed planting is most effective.

| *R. pseudochrysanthum* | APRIL | 0° |
| Barbatum series | Pink | Medium |

Perfect, mound-like growth habit with leaves in stiff rosettes. Young growth covered with woolly indumentum. Flowers are dark pink in bud and open to a good tight truss with crimson spots inside the throat.

| *R. racemosum* | APRIL | −10° |
| Virgatum series | White, pink, deep rose | Semi-dwarf |

There are forms available from dwarf to tall. An intermediate one with a good pink color is most attractive. The name refers to the manner of flowering in racemes from axillary buds.

| *R. smirnowii* | MAY | −15° |
| Ponticum series | Rose, light red | Medium |

A good foliage plant with fawn-colored indumentum. The new shoots of a woolly blue-gray are most interesting. The plant is remarkably free from insect pests. Flowers are rounded trusses with frilled margins. Page 110.

| *R. strigillosum* | APRIL | +10° |
| Barbatum series | Scarlet | Tall |

This species is characteristic of the series with stiff bristles on its leaf stalks. The long, bell-shaped flowers are exceptionally brilliant. Page 130.

R. williamsianum	APRIL	−5°
Thomsonii series	Pink	Dwarf

One of the finest of the species, with small rounded leaves of bright green, this plant is ideal for a rockery. The new growth is a bronze color which adds to the attractiveness. The bell-shaped flowers hang in groups of two and three florets. Best to grow in partial sun to encourage more flower bud production. Protect from late frosts which damage the new growth. Page 55.

R. yakusimanum	MAY	−20°
Ponticum series	Rose, pink, white	Dwarf

Highly prized for its ornamental value, this relatively new plant has created an unprecedented demand. It has small narrow leaves, down-curved with a heavy brown woolly indumentum. The new shoots are also extremely attractive with a whitish, soft down appearance. Interesting trusses resemble appleblossoms. Page 80.

Hybrids

When rhododendrons were first introduced to the landscape, probably about 160 years ago, the huge estates of the time popularized the large species. There are a number of dwarf and medium-size species, however, which offer attractive foliage, color and compact form.

Over the years, rhododendron breeders have concentrated on desirable characteristics to produce a plant acceptable for all phases of landscaping, with emphasis on modern garden architecture. Results have been astounding! Large flowers; wide range of intense colors; lovely form; magnificent, closely-set foliage; greater number of varieties with specified hardiness; plants adaptable to very warm climates; longer-lasting blooms; and other favorable qualities have been developed.

Because of this specialized breeding, it is possible to design rhododendrons for use in almost every landscape situation. The home gardener often finds it easier to match a hybrid rather than a species to his individual needs. Only a few propagators have been producing species rhododendrons and they are not always easy to locate. Most garden centers and retail nurserymen prefer to offer named hybrid varieties because of the greater demand for them. I predict a change in this situation in the future.

The preference for hybrids over species in the past, also results from the belief that some species are more difficult to handle. Frederick Street, famed English nurseryman, gardener and author, claims that species require a rich soil and heavy supply of moisture at all times, and greater selectivity as to location in the landscape. But, the gardener with ample space, wishing to extend his experience with rhododendrons for the sake of scientific knowledge, curiosity or pure joy, will find growing species plants very rewarding.

The balance of this chapter contains a list of hybrid rhododendrons, which I believe offers a wide range of color, form, foliage and hardiness. Some of the most popular varieties grown today are included, along with others presently not so well known but which, I am sure, will become popular, and a few which are so unusual that they excite the imagination. Many were hybridized by famous people in the rhododendron world. There are other worthy varieties, to be sure, but I believe you will be happy if you choose from this list those which fit your climatic situation, and then proceed to follow good cultural practices. Page references indicate color illustrations.

A. BEDFORD	LATE MAY	−5°
Mauve seedling x *ponticum*	Blue	Tall

You will be enchanted with the wide, dark, glossy green foliage. Its height is in keeping with the large foliage and excellent trusses of 14 to 16 flowers. Page 2.

ALADDIN   JUNE   0°
griersonianum x *auriculatum*   Pink   Tall

 Excellent where a tall rhodie is needed in the landscape. It is especially welcome in a garden where heat tolerance is necessary, for it does well in full sun.

ALBERT CLOSE   JUNE   −10°
maximum x *macrophyllum*   Rose   Medium

 Its blue-green leaves make it a delight to connoisseurs who appreciate foliage color. It takes heat well, and I like the compactness of the conical trusses. Page 22.

ALBUM ELEGANS   JUNE   −20°
catawbiense hybrid   White   Tall

 Do not overlook this variety where cold winters are a factor. Gardeners always love the lilac tinge of the white flowers and the rounded trusses. Page 14.

ALICE   EARLY MAY −5°
griffithianum hybrid   Pink   Medium

 Although the foliage will take full sun, the plant should be located so that the flowers will receive some shade. Its deep pink blossoms fade to rose. Page 36.

AMERICA   LATE MAY −25°
Parsons Grandiflorum x dark red hybrid Red   Medium

 Flowers are not too large but of a very good dark red. The ball-type trusses enhance the flower beauty. The best plant habit develops in full sun. Wonderfully hardy. Page VIII.

AMY   EARLY MAY −5°
griffithianum hybrid   Pink   Medium

 If you want a rhododendron that will grow in full sun and really take the heat, this variety is a good choice. You will like the compact trusses of rose-pink flowers.

ANAH KRUSCHKE   LATE MAY −10°
Purple Splendour x *ponticum*   Blue   Medium

 Calling all Los Angeles area rhododendron lovers! This one is for you. It likes full sun and is a plant of beautiful growth. Trusses are tight and conical. Page 56.

ANNA BALDSIEFEN   EARLY APRIL −10°
Pioneer x Pioneer   Pink   Dwarf

 The light rose flowers, slightly ruffled and sporting a darker midrib, will excite your fancy. A lovely miniature with leaves only fingernail size.

ANNA ROSE WHITNEY   LATE MAY 0°
griersonianum x Countess of Derby Pink   Tall

 You will love the outstanding dull olive green of this highly prized rhodie. Leaves are large, 8 x 3 inches, and you need to give this variety plenty of room. Page 60.

ANNIE DALTON   LATE MAY −10°
(decorum x griersonianum) x America Pink   Medium

 A Gable rhododendron that puts a twist to its leaves for added interest in the landscape. You will enjoy the large, lax trusses. Page 16.

ANNIE E. ENDTZ   LATE MAY 0°
Pink Pearl hybrid   Pink   Medium

 A variety very similar to 'Antoon van Welie'. The flower is a lighter shade and has a little more frill. A dependable grower which inherited its parent's vigor.

ANTOON VAN WELIE   **EARLY MAY**   −5°
Pink Pearl hybrid   Pink   Tall

For those who favor larger trusses. I find the somewhat stiff habit of growth more upright in part shade and spreading in full sun, quite interesting. Page X.

ARTHUR J. IVENS   **EARLY MAY**   −10°
williamsianum x *houlstonii*   Rose   Semi-Dwarf

Although this variety is a little slow to flower, you will be well rewarded when it does. Flowers are bell-shaped, and leaves ovate. You can grow it in full sun.

ATROFLO   **LATE MAY**   −5°
Atrosanguineum x *floccigerum*   Rose   Medium

Another Gable hybrid which you will praise highly because of the dark green, suede-like foliage above, and heavy fawn indumentum below. Flowers have good substance.

ATROSANGUINEUM   **LATE MAY**   −20°
catawbeinse hybrid   Red   Medium

Here is an old reliable rhododendron that is popular in the Eastern U.S. A dark red with good foliage and plant habit.

AUTUMN GOLD   **LATE MAY**   0°
discolor x Fabia   Salmon   Medium

A Van Veen introduction of which I am quite proud. Its salmon-apricot color is distinctive. This rhodie must have very light shade to do its best. Light green leaves 5 x 2 inches. Page 89.

AZOR   **JUNE**   −5°
griersonianum x *discolor*   Pink   Medium

An early June blooming variety which does very well in southern climates when shaded. You will enjoy its spreading, open habit and salmon-pink flowers. Page 74.

BACHER'S GOLD   **LATE MAY**   0°
Unknown Warrior x Fabia   Pink   Medium

A tribute to the late John Bacher who did so much to further the cause of rhododendrons and helped to establish the A. R. S. Test Gardens. A good plant and an interesting, different color.

BEAUFORT   **EARLY MAY**   −15°
Boule de Neige x *fortunei*   White   Medium

Do you enjoy lovely fragrance as I do? Then try 'Beaufort'. And it has another important quality; it is not susceptible to lace wing fly.

BEAUTY OF LITTLEWORTH   **EARLY MAY**   −5°
campanulatum x *griffithianum*   White   Tall

Although slow to set buds while a young plant, the wait is well worthwhile once you see the mauve pink buds and highly built-up, large trusses with 16 or 19 flowers. Pages 26 and 131.

BELLE HELLER   **EARLY MAY**   −10°
Catawbiense Album x white *catawbiense* hybrid   White   Medium

If you like an exceptionally bright white, this is your variety. It grows vigorously and every gardener praises the conspicuous golden blotch in the flowers. Page 111.

BESSE HOWELLS   **LATE APRIL**   −20°
Red *catawbiense* hybrid x Boule de Neige   Red   Low

Compact in habit and with excellent lustrous green foliage. It blooms prolifically with ruffled red flowers accented by a dark red blotch. Page 131.

BETTY WORMALD　　　　　　　　　EARLY MAY　　−5°
George Hardy x red hybrid　　　　　Pink　　　Medium

　　Everyone has some favorites. If you live in the south, this could well be one of yours. The plant is upright and spreading, with flowers having a lighter center and a dark blotch on the upper petal. Page 58.

BIBIANI　　　　　　　　　　　　LATE APRIL　　+10°
Moser's Maroon x *arboreum*　　　　Red　　　Tall

　　For a good warm-weather variety 'Bibiani' is hard to beat, but it should be given shelter from the wind. You will enjoy the bright scarlet flowers.

BLAZE　　　　　　　　　　　　　EARLY MAY　　−20°
Mars x *catawbiense* var. *rubrum*　　Red　　　Medium

　　There is no blue in the dark red pyramidal truss with a faint orange-yellow spotting. A robust plant with upright, but not open habit. A fine new hybrid by David Leach.

BLUE DIAMOND　　　　　　　　　EARLY APRIL　　0°
Intrifast x *augustinii*　　　　　　Blue　　　Low

　　Whenever I name the better blues, I include this variety. It is most attractive in a sunny location where its small, distinctive foliage is a delightful contrast. Pages 17, 49 and 62.

BLUE ENSIGN　　　　　　　　　　LATE MAY　　−10°
ponticum hybrid　　　　　　　　　Blue　　　Medium

　　Similar to 'Blue Peter' but you will particularly like its better growth habit and smaller, less droopy leaves. Pages 126 and front cover.

BLUE JAY　　　　　　　　　　　JUNE　　　−5°
ponticum hybrid　　　　　　　　　Blue　　　Medium

　　Noted for its exceptional form and bright green foliage that remains on the plant for a number of years. The blue flower has a brown blotch above.

BLUE PETER　　　　　　　　　　EARLY MAY　　−10°
ponticum hybrid　　　　　　　　　Blue　　　Medium

　　Truly one of the old reliables. Light lavender blue flowers that have frilled margins and make conical, compact trusses. The leaves are dark, glossy green. Pages 17 and 68.

BLUE RIVER　　　　　　　　　　LATE APRIL　　−5°
Van Nes Sensation x Emperor de Maroc　Blue　　　Medium

　　A brand new variety with flowers of an exciting soft blue shade. I believe it will become a favorite of gardeners in the South.

BLUE TIT　　　　　　　　　　　EARLY APRIL　　0°
impeditum x *augustinii*　　　　　Blue　　Semi-dwarf

　　Another old timer with a compact growth habit. The flowers are actually a light greyish blue and are extremely profuse. I am fond of its small leaves. Page 30.

BOULE DE NEIGE　　　　　　　　LATE APRIL　　−25°
caucasicum x *catawbiense* hybrid　White　　　Low

　　This very hardy and vigorous plant should be grown in the shade to combat the lace wing fly. The flowers make compact, rounded trusses. Page 31.

BOULE DE ROSE　　　　　　　　LATE APRIL　　−20°
Red *catawbiense* hybrid x Boule de Neige　Pink　　Medium

　　Following closely the habit of 'Boule de Neige', this new hybrid grows to about four feet and then extends outward indefinitely in a dense, compact mound. A bright rose-pink with a slight brownish flare on the upper lobe.

| BOW BELLS | EARLY MAY | 0° |
| Corona x *williamsianum* | Pink | Low |

A real "must" for the landscape and always popular. The flowers are cup-shape and held in a lax truss. You will love the copper-bronze color of the new growth. Page 10.

| BRIC-A-BRAC | FEBRUARY | +5° |
| *leucaspis* x *moupinense* | White | Semi-dwarf |

A bearer of very early flowers that are so welcome during the late winter. The blooms are doubly interesting because of their chocolate anthers. Dark green leaves.

| BRITANNIA | LATE MAY | −5° |
| Queen Wilhelmina x Stanley Davies | Red | Medium |

It is not contradictory to call this plant spreading and compact, since it is both. The flowers are bright scarlet, bell-shaped and borne in medium round trusses.

| BROUGHTONII AUREUM | LATE MAY | 0° |
| (*maximum* x *ponticum*) x *molle* | Yellow | Low |

One of the best of the azaleodendrons. The foliage is semi-deciduous and the soft-yellow flowers are dotted with orange-yellow. Somewhat heat tolerant. Page 129.

| BURGUNDY | LATE APRIL | −5° |
| Britannia x Purple Splendour | Red | Medium |

Californians, this new variety is certainly one you should try. Unusual flower color, good foliage, excellent growth habit and "growability" recommend it.

| BUTTERFLY | EARLY MAY | 0° |
| *campylocarpum* x Mrs. Milner | Yellow | Medium |

Good heat tolerance makes this rhodie popular where that quality is a necessity, plus the fact that it can also be grown successfully in shade. Red flecking on the flowers adds much interest. Page 50.

| CADIS | LATE MAY | −15° |
| Caroline x *discolor* | Pink | Medium |

A Gable hybrid with very fragrant, large flowers which attract gardeners and garden visitors. Give it some sun if you want it to flower well. Page 69.

| CALSTOCKER | LATE APRIL | 0° |
| *calophytum* x Dr. Stocker | White | Tall |

A variety which grows taller than it does wide and certainly fits certain landscape situations. Although pink in bud, the flowers open to huge, dome-shaped, white trusses.

| CANDIDISSIMUM | JUNE | −15° |
| *catawbiense* hybrid | White | Medium |

Although not a new introduction, it is rather rare, and you may have trouble locating a plant. It has lovely blush white trusses framed by dark green leaves.

| CAPTAIN JACK | LATE MAY | +5° |
| Mars x *eriogynum* | Red | Tall |

Do you like names that awaken the imagination? This one does, and so will the outstanding dark red color of the blooms. The flowers measure 3½ inches across, 15 to a truss.

| CARACTACUS | JUNE | −25° |
| *catawbiense* hybrid | Red | Medium |

This is known as one of the ironclads, those varieties which do well where the weather gets really cold, and I think it deserves a better rating than it sometimes gets.

CARITA   LATE APRIL   +5°
Naomi x *campylocarpum*   Yellow   Medium

A good variety with dome-shaped trusses that bear 12 to 13 flowers. It needs some shade from hot sun. Clones are 'Carita Inchmery' and 'Golden Dream'. Page 79.

CARMEN   EARLY MAY   −5°
didymum x *forrestii* var. *repens*   Red   Dwarf

Certainly one of the best dwarves but to perform properly it must have excellent drainage. 'Carmen' grows slowly but is very sturdy. The leaves are a handsome dark green. Page 41.

CAROLINE   LATE MAY   −15°
decorum hybrid   Lavender   Medium

A Gable hybrid with a delightful fragrance. It does very well in hot climates, and is quite resistant to *phytophthora* root rot. Page 44.

CAROLYN GRACE   LATE APRIL   +5°
wardii hybrid   Yellow   Medium

I believe this hybrid is a bit hardier than indicated. The 3½-inch flowers are wide, shallow, campanulate and of good substance. The foliage is shiny and medium green.

CARY ANN   EARLY MAY   −5°
Corona x Vulcan   Red   Low

If you are looking for a good, heavy-flowered red which is completely at home in full sun, try this variety. Sunken veins add to the appeal of its leaves. Page 25.

CATAWBIENSE ALBUM   LATE MAY   −25°
catawbiense selection   White   Medium

Another "hardy-as-an-oak" type which can certainly take the cold. The buds are a flushed lilac, and the foliage is a medium dark green. It does well under many growing conditions. Page 55.

CATAWBIENSE BOURSAULT   LATE MAY   −20°
catawbiense selection   Purple   Tall

Some call the blossoms a rose-lilac, although I list them as a purple. Either way, it is a fine plant with a good growing habit and sturdy constitution.

CATAWBIENSE GRANDIFLORUM   LATE MAY   −15°
catawbiense selection   Lilac   Tall

The color of this selection is sufficiently distinctive to make it very attractive. You will like its long-lasting flowers. Page 4.

CHARLES DICKENS   LATE MAY   −25°
catawbiense hybrid   Red   Medium

Slow growing but very hardy and well worth having in the landscape. The flowers are purplish crimson carried in full conical trusses. Dark green foliage gives pleasure the year around.

CHEER   EARLY APRIL   −10°
Red *catawbiense* hybrid x Cunningham's White   Pink   Low

A compact, medium-dwarf plant which is covered generously with foliage. It is a real showpiece with its shell-pink flowers splashed with conspicuous scarlet-red blotches. Page 4.

CHEVALIER FELIX DE SAUVAGE   LATE APRIL   −5°
caucasicum x hardy hybrid   Red   Low

If you have a greenhouse, try forcing this hybrid. Blotches on the upper flower petals enhance their beauty. The plant is broadly spreading in habit. Page 19.

CHINA   EARLY MAY   0°
wightii x *fortunei*   Yellow   Tall

   To me, the foliage of 'China' is one of the handsomest among the rhodie
hybrids. Deep within the pale cream flowers lies a red blotch. Grow this variety
in the open or in light shade.

CHIONOIDES   LATE MAY   −15°
ponticum hybrid   White   Low

   This is one of the best of the whites that have a low growing habit. It produces a good bushy plant which landscapers always find valuable in their designs. Page 51.

CHRISTMAS CHEER   MARCH   −5°
caucasicum hybrid   Pink   Low

   Another winter blooming hybrid which brings you that welcome early color
in the garden. The pink buds fade to very light pink flowers, and the plant
stands considerable sun. Page 81.

CILPINENSE   MARCH   +5°
ciliatum x *moupinense*   Pink   Semi-dwarf

   For late winter garden color, try 'Cilpinense'. Give it some protection at
blooming time to prevent frost injury. Its leaves are a lovely shiny green.
Page 18.

C.I.S.   EARLY MAY   +10°
Loder's White x Fabia   Yellow   Medium

   "Biscuit" best describes this flower color. The 4-inch florets have a brilliant
orange-red throat. The leaf tips twist distinctively. Be sure you provide light
shade. Page 57.

CLEMENTINE LEMAIRE   LATE MAY   0°
Unknown   Pink   Medium

   If you are intrigued by unusual varieties as I am, then you will want this one.
It has tight, rounded trusses of pink flowers, each blotched with yellow.

CONEMAUGH   MARCH   −15°
racemosum x *mucronulatum*   Pink   Low

   A small, semi-deciduous and most interesting variety. The lovely star-shaped
flowers make lavender-pink trusses only 2 inches in diameter.

CONEWAGO   EARLY APRIL   −25°
carolinianum x *mucronulatum*   Pink   Low

   You will find this growth pattern different: Long branches radiate from its
base forming a fairly open plant. 'Conewago Improved' is very floriferous.

CORNUBIA   MARCH   +15°
arboreum x Shilsonii   Red   Tall

   A real favorite of gardeners who live in the San Francisco Bay area. The
slight prominences on the medium green leaves add much interest. Flowers
are a blood red. Page 105.

CORONA   LATE MAY   −5°
Unknown   Pink   Medium

   Coral-pink flowers combine with compact, roundish, upright branches to
form a truly distinctive variety. Pest resistance is good, as is its heat tolerance.

COTTON CANDY   EARLY MAY   0°
Marinus Koster x Loderi Venus   Pink   Medium

   Introduced by John Henny, another hybridist who gave so much to the
rhododendron world. The foliage is dark green and the soft pink flowers are
borne in tall compact trusses. Page 104.

COUNTESS OF DERBY   EARLY MAY   −5°
Pink Pearl x Cynthia   Pink   Medium

You find this variety being sold as 'Eureka Maid' in the U.S. Flowers start rose-pink and gradually fade to a pale pink. The habit is open and spreading. Page 30.

COUNTESS OF HADDINGTON   EARLY APRIL   +20°
ciliatum x dalhousiae   Pink   Medium

Blooms prolifically after it has become well established. I suggest you give it half shade. You will appreciate its ornamental value and its fragrance.

COUNTY OF YORK   EARLY MAY   −15°
Catawbiense Album x Loderi King George   White   Tall

On my list this is rated as a good, hardy variety. Long, dark green, convex leaves frame the pale chartreuse buds and olive-throated flowers. Pages 64 and 76.

CREAM CREST   EARLY APRIL   0°
chryseum x Cilpinense   Yellow   Low

This light yellow contrasts beautifully with the blue dwarf types. Borne in a tight truss are 6 to 8 cup-shaped flowers. The small leaves are most attractive. Page 54.

CREST   EARLY MAY   −5°
wardii x Lady Bessborough   Yellow   Tall

Propagators find this hybrid difficult to root, and it holds its leaves only one year, but the Rothschild rhodie comes nearest to a true yellow. Good upright growth.

CRIMSON GLORY   LATE MAY   −10°
Unknown   Red   Medium

Gardeners always enjoy the crimson red blooms which are produced even by young plants. The flowers are long-lasting and the plant shape is good. Page 98.

CUNNINGHAM'S WHITE   LATE MAY   −15°
caucasicum x ponticum var. *album*   White   Semi-dwarf

Reputedly grows well in neutral to slightly alkaline soil. It will take full exposure but does best in partial shade. A yellowish blotch enhances the white flower. Page 22.

CUTIE   LATE APRIL   −15°
calostrotum hybrid   Pink   Dwarf

Once called 'Calostrotum Pink' but its present name is more descriptive. An upright, rounded plant, wider than tall, with pink blossoms shaded lilac. Page 24.

CYNTHIA   LATE MAY   −10°
catawbiense x griffithianum   Rose   Tall

One of the best known rhodies and a perennial favorite of gardeners. It is vigorous and tall. Grows openly in shade but compactly in full sun. Medium dark green foliage. Page 71.

DAMOZEL   LATE MAY   0°
griersonianum hybrid   Red   Tall

This is a fine variety for the Southeast. Somewhat open, spreading habit. The bright red flowers, spotted darker, are nestled among handsome, dark green, narrow leaves.

143

DAPHNOIDES LATE MAY −10°
virgatum hybrid Purple Low

A rare variety which certainly would fit well in California landscaping. Its foliage is distinctive in color and the plant rounded in form. Flower color is bright. Page 98.

DAVID EARLY MAY +5°
Hugh Koster x *neriiflorum* Red Tall

The deep blood red flowers are very rich and distinctive. The blossoms last longer in partial shade but the plant will thrive in full sun. The dark green foliage is good looking. Page 31 and back cover.

DAVID GABLE EARLY MAY −15°
Atrosanguineum x *fortunei* Pink Medium

A Gable hybrid I am sure you will like for its fine plant habit, large leaves and red-throated pink flowers. It is filled with dome-shaped flower trusses. Page 91.

DEVONSHIRE CREAM EARLY MAY 0°
campylocarpum hybrid Yellow Semi-dwarf

The ball-type trusses of creamy yellow flowers always attract attention. And when you need a very compact plant, you will find this variety among the best.

DIDO LATE MAY 0°
dichroanthum x *decorum* Orange Low

Another good compact rhododendron with sturdy, low growth. I am very fond of its orange-yellow flowers of tubular shape and of the manner they are borne in lax trusses.

DISCA JUNE −10°
discolor x Caroline White Medium

Valuable for its fragrance, fine habit of growth and vigor. The slightly frilled white flowers are tinged pink. 'Disca' prefers light shade. Page 88.

DONCASTER EARLY MAY −5°
arboreum hybrid Red Semi-dwarf

I heartily recommend this variety for warm weather localities. Handsome dark green leaves, 6 x 2 inches, and crimson scarlet flowers adorn the open spreading plant.

DORA AMATEIS LATE APRIL −15°
carolinianum x *ciliatum* White Semi-dwarf

For a free flowering, rather compact plant 'Dora Amateis' is hard to beat. It is vigorous and easily grown. Interesting green spots enliven the white flowers. Page 16.

DOUBLOONS EARLY MAY 0°
Carolyn Grace x Moonstone Yellow Semi-dwarf

I think you will like this new hybrid. The funnel-shaped flowers are deep yellow and 3 inches across. Blue-green, roundish foliage is carried on a compact rounded plant.

DR. A. BLOK EARLY MAY −5°
Pink Pearl x *catawbiense* Pink Tall

I find the big buds and large leaves fascinating. The pink flowers fade lighter at the center with a pale yellow touch on the upper petals. Page 32.

DR. STOCKER LATE APRIL +5°
caucasicum x *griffithianum* White Medium

The open, campanulate flowers, 3 inches across, are a waxy, ivory white and borne in well rounded trusses. The leaves are medium green and elliptical. A rather pest resistant variety.

144

DR. V. H. RUTGERS   LATE MAY   −15°
Charles Dickens x Lord Roberts   Red   Medium

Imagine fringed flowers of aniline red, dark green leaves and a plant which is broad and dense. This will give you a idea of 'Dr. V. H. Rutgers'. Page 66.

EARL OF ATHLONE   LATE APRIL   0°
Queen Wilhelmina x Stanley Davies   Red   Medium

You will enjoy the bright blood red of the bell-like flowers. I believe this plant has one of the finest trusses among the red rhodies. It is compact and dome-shaped.

EDWARD DUNN   LATE MAY   +5°
discolor x (*dichroanthum* x *neriiflorum*)   Yellow   Medium

Named for one of the most enthusiastic rhododendron people, it has flowers of apricot-pink carried in a dome-shaped truss. The plant grows best in partial shade.

EDWARD S. RAND   LATE MAY   −15°
catawbiense hybrid   Red   Medium

A distinctive bronze eye lies in each crimson red flower. The foliage is a yellowish green and forms a plant which is quite compact.

EL ALAMEIN   EARLY MAY   −10°
griffithianum hybrid   Red   Medium

This was introduced by the Dutch hybridist Kluis, and it looks like a winner. Deep red flowers blotched with brown form an almost ideal truss.

ELDORADO   EARLY APRIL   +10°
valentinianum x *johnstoneanum*   Yellow   Low

The funnel-shaped flowers are very yellow and made even more attractive by the brown scales on the outside. And I like the scaly, dark yellowish-green leaves.

ELIE   EARLY APRIL   −10°
Pink *catawbiense* hybrid x Pink *catawbiense* hyrid   Pink   Medium

Surely you will agree that its lustrous dark green foliage is extremely handsome. The plant is compact and dotted with numerous vibrant deep pink flowers accented by a cerise red blotch. Page 75.

ELISABETH HOBBIE   EARLY APRIL   −10°
Essex Scarlet x *forrestii* var. *repens*   Red   Semi-dwarf

One of the famed Hobbie hybrids. The tight growing habit, nicely textured, glossy dark green leaves and brilliant scarlet red flowers all recommend it highly. Page 130.

ELIZABETH   EARLY APRIL   0°
forrestii var. *repens* x *griersonianum*   Red   Low

Imagine the reddest of reds and you are close to the color of 'Elizabeth'. Its leaves are dark green above and glaucous beneath with a bit of indumentum. Six to eight flowers per truss. Page 72.

ELIZABETH TITCOMB   LATE APRIL   0°
Marinus Koster x Snow Queen   Pink   Medium

Dark pink margin etches pale pink flowers of excellent substance, all carried in conical trusses. A fine sturdy plant for full sun.

ELSE FRYE   MARCH   +15°
ciliicalyx hybrid   Pink   Medium

Most unusual coloring, for the white flowers are flushed pink-rose with a chrome-yellow throat lying deep within. The loose truss has three to six flowers. Bristled foliage on a robust plant. Page 78.

| ELSPETH | EARLY MAY | 0° |
| *campylocarpum* x hardy hybrid | Apricot | Low |

Another unusual flower which is bright scarlet in bud, deep pink-apricot as it opens, fading to cream. Compact plant with light green foliage.

| ERMINE | LATE MAY | 0° |
| Britannia x Mrs. A. T. de la Mare | White | Medium |

These tall, well-filled trusses of pure white will certainly go well in almost any landscape. 'Ermine' is sturdy and grows well in full sun. Medium green leaves.

| ETHEL | EARLY MAY | +5° |
| F. C. Puddle x *forrestii* var. *repens* | Red | Dwarf |

A very few rhodies have a delightful spreading, creeping habit, and this is one of the best. It has crimson-scarlet, bell-shaped flowers, borne three to five in a truss.

| EVENING GLOW | LATE MAY | 0° |
| *discolor* x Fabia | Yellow | Medium |

Mr. Van Veen was most pleased with this hybrid. Its flowers are a bright yellow with a prominent calyx and carried in lax trusses. The leaves are light green. Page 19.

| EVERESTIANUM | LATE MAY | −15° |
| *catawbiense* hybrid | Rosy-lilac | Tall |

My commendations for this one include pest resistance, heavy flowering, and the fact that it does well in either sun or light shade. Its spotted, rosy-lilac flowers flaunt frilled edges.

| FABIA | LATE MAY | +10° |
| *dichroanthum* x *griersonianum* | Orange | Low |

There are several named forms of this one but I do not think you will find a one lacking thrilling color. With its beautiful indumentum on the foliage and loose hanging, bell-like flowers, this variety offers something different for the landscape. Page 72.

| FAGGETTER'S FAVOURITE | LATE APRIL | 0° |
| *fortunei* hybrid | Pink | Tall |

To put it simply, this is a wonderful rhododendron. Large dark green leaves accentuate fragrant, flushed-pink flowers with speckled brown throats. Page 7.

| FASTUOSUM PLENUM | EARLY MAY | −10° |
| *catawbiense* x *ponticum* | Lavender | Tall |

Charming, semi-double flowers such as these are rare in rhododendrons. The slightly convex leaves are dark green above, light green below. Plant in half shade to prolong flowering. Page 28.

| FAWN | EARLY MAY | +5° |
| *fortunei* x Fabia | Salmon pink | Tall |

The flowers are a thrilling salmon pink, shading to orange-yellow in the center and measuring up to 5 inches across! The corolla is very flat and the truss cylindrical with an open top.

| FAYETTA | EARLY MAY | +5° |
| Tally Ho x Golden Horn | Red | Semi-dwarf |

Be assured that this one is filled with hose-in-hose flowers of purest bright red. You undoubtedly will also like its unusual, dark green leaves.

| FORSTERIANUM | EARLY MAY | +5° |
| *veitchianum* x *edgeworthii* | White | Medium |

Not as fragrant as 'Fragrantissimum' but a better garden plant because of its more upright and compact habit. A truss contains three or four five-inch funnel-shaped flowers with a conspicuous yellow flare.

146

FRAGRANTISSIMUM
edgeworthii x *formosum*
EARLY APRIL +20°
White Medium

For fragrance, don't miss this one which has a delightful nutmeg scent. Buds are flushed carmine, opening to pure white funnel-shaped flowers up to 4 inches wide.

FULL MOON
Crest x Harvest Moon
EARLY MAY −5°
Yellow Low

Gardeners love the prominently veined, bright green leaves. Ball type trusses are compacted with waxy, deep canary-yellow flowers. The plant is one of John Henny's introductions.

GENERAL EISENHOWER
griffithianum hybrid
EARLY MAY 0°
Red Medium

A worthy plant named for a great American. The flowers of deep carmine red are large and ruffled. It is compact and excellent for low profile landscaping. Page 122.

GIGANTEUM
catawbiense hybrid
EARLY MAY −15°
Red Medium

Another hardy oldtimer good for the colder climates. Foliage is dark green and the flowers are light crimson. Do not confuse it with the species of the same name. Page 99.

GILL'S CRIMSON
griffithianum hybrid
EARLY APRIL +10°
Red Tall

An early flowering rhodie which has rather long lasting, blood crimson flowers with good substance. The truss is dome-shaped, flat-topped and tight. Light green foliage.

GIPSY KING
haematodes x King George
LATE MAY +5°
Red Low

With a name like that, it has to be a fine red. The flowers are waxy and the growth is compact and low for those special landscape situations.

GOLDEN BELLE
discolor x Fabia
LATE MAY 0°
Apricot Low

Truly fascinating are the saucer-shaped, large flowers with their yellow centers and deep pink edges. You will like its compact, low, spreading habit. Will do best under partial shade.

GOLDFORT
Goldsworth Yellow x *fortunei*
LATE MAY −10°
Yellow Medium

'Goldfort' is a member of that rare class of rhodies which are yellow and can also stand cold much below zero. The flower color is a clear pale yellow, melting to greenish yellow in the center. Page 127.

GOLD MOHUR
Day Dream x Margaret Dunn
LATE MAY +5°
Yellow Medium

This variety has not been on the market too long. It is a nice yellow with quite good habit.

GOLDSWORTH CRIMSON
griffithianum x hardy hybrid
EARLY MAY 0°
Red Medium

Rounded trusses of bright crimson bloom freely. A spreading but compact plant with long, narrow leaves. Black spotting on the upper petals. The other parent is probably 'Doncaster'. Page 24.

GOLDSWORTH ORANGE
dichroanthum x *discolor*
LATE MAY −5°
Orange Medium

Funnel-shaped flowers, pale orange and uniquely tinged pink, lay in lax trusses. Hybridists often use it in crossing for yellow. Does its best in shade.

GOLDSWORTH YELLOW   LATE MAY   −15°
Jacksonii x *campylocarpum*   Yellow   Medium

The apricot buds open into nice trusses of buff yellow, dotted with bronze on the upper lobe. Note the degree of hardiness! I believe it is better than rated by the ARS. Pages 38 and 125.

GOMER WATERER   LATE MAY   −15°
catawbiense hybrid   White   Medium

Frothy masses of delicate rose-tinged flowers turning to blush white and glossy dark green leaves make this an attractive plant the year around. It is heat and sun tolerant, and I find it easy to grow. Page 20.

GRAF ZEPPELIN   LATE MAY   −5°
Pink Pearl x Mrs. C. S. Sargent   Pink   Medium

You may have difficulty in finding this variety but it is worth the search. A vigorous grower with coarse, dark glossy foliage framing the bright pink flowers. Page 87.

GREAT LAKES   EARLY MAY   −25°
catawbiense var. *album* 'Glass' x *yakusimanum*   White   Semi-dwarf

Those of you living in cold climates, note that hardiness! Leaves are made more interesting by the thin tan indumentum. Pink buds become white flowers. Sun tolerant.

GRETCHEN   EARLY MAY   −15°
(*decorum* x *griffithianum*) x Kettledrum Pink   Medium

You will like the plant habit, fine foliage and large dome-shaped trusses. It is very floriferous, bearing red-throated, pink blossoms.

GRIEROSPLENDOUR   LATE MAY   0°
griersonianum x Purple Splendour   Plum   Low

Californians like this hybrid. The younger upright growth becomes spreading when older. It produces red-purple flowers when still quite young.

GROSCLAUDE   LATE MAY   +5°
haematodes x *eriogynum*   Red   Low

Look carefully at its brown indumentum. Note its compactness and light green, recurved leaves. Check its waxy, heavy-textured, bell-shaped bright scarlet flowers. You will like it.

HARVEST MOON   EARLY MAY   0°
Mrs. Lindsay Smith x *campylocarpum* hybrid Yellow   Medium

My eye is always caught by this one's slightly-bullate, shiny, yellow-green leaves. But I also enjoy the pale yellow flowers spotted with red. Page 102.

HELENE SCHIFFNER   EARLY MAY   −5°
Unknown   White   Low

From bud to open flower, this is pure white, without a touch of spotting. The dome-shaped trusses are attractive as are the upward-folded and pointed leaves. Page 83.

HENRIETTA SARGENT   LATE MAY   −25°
catawbiense hybrid   Rose pink   Medium

With its large, dome-shaped truss, the flower is similar to that of 'Mrs. C. S. Sargent.' But it is a lower grower and suitable for different landscape situations. Page 108.

HOLDEN   LATE APRIL   −15°
Red *catawbiense* seedling x Cunningham's White Red   Medium

A good compact plant with lustrous dark green foliage I'm sure you will like. A small, dark red blotch illuminates the rose-red flower. Page 124.

HONEYMOON LATE APRIL −5°
Devonshire Cream x *wardii* Yellow Low

Chartreuse-yellow flowers completely cover the plant. I love its heart-shaped, dark, glossy foliage and dense rounded form. Truly a remarkable plant.

HUMMING BIRD LATE APRIL 0°
haematodes x *williamsianum* Red Semi-dwarf

As delightful as its name. Medium red flowers, borne in lax trusses, have very heavy substance. Does best when planted in some shade.

HURRICANE EARLY MAY −5°
Anna Rose Whitney x Mrs. Furnival Pink Medium

A 1969 release with tight, rounded trusses of pink flowers splashed with sienna on the upper corolla. Large dark green leaves make it an excellent year-around plant. Page 118.

ICE CUBE EARLY MAY −20°
Catalgla x Belle Heller White Medium

Ivory white flowers enhanced by a lemon blotch are carried on well formed trusses. Large dark green foliage fills out the plant very well. Page 35.

IDEALIST LATE APRIL +5°
wardii x Naomi Yellow Medium

'Naomi' type foliage with vigorous upright habit. The wide campanulate flowers are a light yellow slightly tinged with green. Some shade is best. Page 97.

IGNATIUS SARGENT LATE MAY −25°
catawbiense hybrid Rose Medium

Look at this hardiness for gardens that need it. The large, deep rose flowers are slightly scented. Habit of growth is open. Page 99.

ILAM VIOLET LATE APRIL 0°
Electra x *russatum* Violet Low

This plant from New Zealand boasts of being one of the best flowering clear violets. The growth habit and foliage make an excellent landscape subject. Page 36.

JAN DEKENS EARLY MAY 0°
Unknown Pink Tall

The lovely trusses, upright and tight, and the bold foliage are really recommendation enough. But large ruffled bright pink flowers edged by deeper pink make this plant a true bonanza in beauty. Page 41.

JANET BLAIR EARLY MAY −15°
Dexter hybrid x unknown parent Pink Tall

A new David Leach introduction destined to become a favorite. A golden flare adds sparkle to the large fimbriated flowers of pastel mauve. Page 82.

JEAN MARIE DE MONTAGUE EARLY MAY 0°
griffithianum hybrid Red Low

You may find this listed as The Honorable Jean Marie de Montague. A very popular Northwest standard with good eastern success. Bright scarlet flowers, attractive dark green foliage and compact habit. Pages 21 and 62.

J. H. VAN NES EARLY MAY 0°
Monsieur Thiers x *griffithianum* hybrid Red Medium

A good soft red which fades to a paler hue in the center. Pointed lobes are carried in conical, compact truss. Avoid over-fertilization. Page 82.

JINGLE BELLS   EARLY MAY   0°
Ole Olson x Fabia   Yellow   Semi-dwarf

One of the newer varieties showing great promise. It features good compactness with shining dark green leaves. Tubular flowers are a pleasing blend of rose, orange and yellow. Page 132.

JOCK   LATE APRIL   −5°
williamsianum x *griersonianum*   Pink   Low

Will do best in full sun. I am sure you will like its dark pink, slightly blushed flowers which are made more appealing by a faint orange throat.

JOHN COUTTS   LATE MAY   +5°
(Grand Arab x *griffithianum*) x *griersonianum*   Pink   Medium

Long pointed leaves set off the smooth, large flowers of salmon pink with a deeper colored throat. The habit is dense. Foliage will easily burn in the sun.

JOHN WALTER   LATE MAY   −10°
catawbiense x *arboreum*   Red   Medium

This variety buds easily, producing ruffled flowers of crimson red. The growth is compact and the leaves are dark green. Page 63.

KATE WATERER   LATE MAY   −10°
catawbiense hybrid   Pink   Medium

I like the golden eye sparkling within the pink flowers. Medium compactness and fairly upright in growth. Page 103.

KENTUCKY CARDINAL   LATE MAY   −5°
brachycarpum x Essex Scarlet   Red   Medium

Dark red flowers, so often wanted in the landscape, with matching dark green leaves. The plant is open in habit.

KING OF SHRUBS   LATE MAY   +5°
discolor x Fabia   Apricot yellow   Medium

Well named, I think, because of its unusual coloring. The base of the flower is an apricot yellow with the inner margin banded porcelain rose. Light green foliage. Page 62.

KING TUT   EARLY MAY   −20°
smirnowii x America   Pink   Medium

Not an Egyptian king but a plant with deep light shaded pink flowers with slight yellowish brown blotches. Excellent plant habit. Foliage is a pea green with an interesting light dusting. Page XII.

KLUIS SENSATION   EARLY MAY   0°
Britannia x unnamed seedling   Red   Low

The flower is similar to 'Jean Marie de Montague' with small, tight trusses. The plant is rather compact. You will like its dark green crinkly leaves. Page 60.

KLUIS TRIUMPH   LATE MAY   0°
griffithianum hybrid   Red   Medium

Be sure to shade from direct sun to protect the smooth metallic deep red trusses. Erect and slightly open habit with good foliage.

LADY ALICE FITZWILLIAM   LATE APRIL   +20°
Unknown   White   Medium

Similar to 'Fragrantissimum' but more bushy and erect. Pink buds burst into fragrant white flowers. Although heat tolerant, it should have half shade. Margins of leaves curl inward.

LADY ARMSTRONG   LATE MAY   −20°
catawbiense hybrid   Pink   Medium

Another good hardy variety with fine rose-pink flowers displaying a white throat.

LADY BERRY   LATE APRIL   +5°
Rosy Bell x Royal Flush   Red   Medium

You must have this variety for its blue-green aromatic leaves. The trusses carry eight tubular flowers that are brilliant jasper red outside, lined with rose opal inside.

LADY BESSBOROUGH   LATE MAY   −5°
discolor x *campylocarpum* var. *elatum* Yellow   Medium

A delicate flower which is highly attractive. The leaves are medium green, the habit upright and open. There are several clones, but as a whole they are a light yellow with deeper color at the base of the throat.

LADY BLIGH   LATE MAY   0°
griffithianum hybrid   Red   Medium

Medium green leaves are held for two years. The flowers, measuring three inches across, begin strawberry and fade to pink. Plant is spreading and rounded, wider than it is tall. Page 42.

LADY CHAMBERLAIN   LATE APRIL   +10°
cinnabarinum var. *roylei* x Royal Flush orange form Various Tall

There are various forms and colors of this variety. The flowers run from bright orange to salmon pink, are tubular and trumpet-shape. Blue-green leaves are waxy.

LADY CLEMENTINE MITFORD   LATE MAY   0°
maximum hybrid   Pink   Medium

A fine hot weather variety which is wider than tall and of medium compact habit. Soft peach flowers, edged darker, fill dome-shaped trusses. The leaves are medium to dark green. Page 53.

LADY ELEANOR CATHCART   LATE MAY   −15°
maximum x *arboreum*   Pink   Tall

Clear pink flowers proudly display a purplish blotch. The plant is rounded and medium compact. A variety which will stand Texas-type heat.

LADY LONGMAN   LATE MAY   −15°
Cynthia x Lady Eleanor Cathcart   Pink   Medium

Large trusses of bold flowers strongly marked with a chocolate eye. Heavily marked leaves. This is a good hot weather variety.

LADY PRIMROSE   EARLY MAY   0°
campylocarpum hybrid   Yellow   Medium

Open flowers are a clear primrose yellow dotted with red. I particularly like the flat yellow buds which are tinged pink. It needs shade for best results.

LADY ROSEBERRY   LATE APRIL   +5°
cinnabarinum var. *roylei* x Royal Flush Pink   Tall

Pink form. New leaves are bluish-green and later turn to a smooth green. The shell pink flowers shade to rose at the base. They are fleshy and tubular, flaring to a funnel shape.

LAMPLIGHTER   EARLY MAY   0°
Britannia x Madame Fr. J. Chauvin   Red   Medium

You cannot help but like the wonderful salmon glow of the red flowers, which are carried in large conical trusses. The leaves are medium green on a compact and rounded plant. Page 128.

LANGLEY PARK   EARLY MAY   0°
Queen Wilhelmina x Stanley Davies   Red   Medium

Bright red flowers are rather thin textured and should have protection from sun to last well. The long leaves are dark green, pointed, and folded along the mid-rib.

LAVENDER GIRL   EARLY MAY   −5°
fortunei x Lady Grey Egerton   Lavender   Medium

A variety which deserves to be more popular. The flowers are almost white, slightly tinged pink. The large, attractive, light green leaves are held for three years. Page II.

LAVENDER QUEEN   LATE APRIL   −10°
Red *catawbiense* seedling x Boule de Neige   Lavender   Medium

This variety certainly has outstanding habit and foliage, the leaves being a shiny, dark green. Slightly ruffled flowers are bluish lavender touched with a faint brown patch.

LEABURG   EARLY APRIL   0°
dichroanthum x Penjerrick   Red   Semi-dwarf

The glossy dark green leaves and brilliant red waxy flowers in flat-topped trusses should place this one high on your list of favorites. It is very compact in habit.

LEE'S BEST PURPLE   JUNE   −20°
catawbiense hybrid   Purple   Tall

This hybrid has excellent glossy, smooth foliage. Quite similar to 'Lee's Dark Purple' in flower.

LEE'S DARK PURPLE   LATE MAY   −15°
catawbiense hybrid   Purple   Tall

After a hundred years, this one is still very popular. It does well in the Southwestern U.S. Dark purple flowers are surrounded by the dark wavy foliage.

LEO   LATE MAY   −5°
Britannia x *elliottii*   Red   Medium

My belief is that this is one of the finest reds, with its waxy flowers of dark cranberry. A wonderful foliage plant with traces of indumentum beneath the leaves. Page 87.

LEONA   EARLY MAY   0°
Corona x Dondis   Pink   Medium

Compare the dome-shaped trusses of rich pink flowers with other pinks. It rates very highly with me. Flowers are large, leaves medium green, and the habit is open.

LETTY EDWARDS   EARLY MAY   0°
campylocarpum var. *elatum* x *fortunei*   Yellow   Medium

Nine to eleven sulfur yellow flowers are carried on rounded trusses. Red-brown petiols add another sprinkling of color. The plant is rounded, and fairly compact with medium green leaves.

LITTLE BERT   LATE APRIL   +10°
forrestii var. *repens* x *euchaites*   Red   Dwarf

Shining crimson scarlet flowers of bell shape hang in rather loose trusses. The leaves are rounded at each end. Page 15.

LITTLE GEM   EARLY MAY   +5°
Carmen x *elliottii*   Red   Dwarf

You will like this charmer for the rockery or border. It is an attractive dwarf with blood red flowers and very different foliage. Page 84.

LODAURIC   JUNE   −5°
Loderi group x *auriculatum*   White   Tall

A late bloomer with trumpet-shaped, white flowers displaying a yellow throat. Crinkled blossoms have a delightful, spicy fragrance. Flowers last quite well in the sun. Vigorous.

LODERI KING GEORGE
griffithianum x *fortunei*

EARLY MAY   0°
White   Tall

A truly outstanding rhododendron. The flowers, pink in bud and opening to white, are large and very fragrant. The open, thick-branched plants need sun and wind protection. Pages 26 and 118.

LODERI PINK DIAMOND
griffithianum x *fortunei*

EARLY MAY   0°
Pink   Tall

This is one of the many clones of 'Loderi' which are the same in habit and foliage as 'Loderi King George'. The flowers, however, are shaded a delicate pink.

LODERI VENUS
griffithianum x *fortunei*

EARLY MAY   0°
Pink   Tall

Another of the 'Loderi' clones. This variety has lovely shell pink flowers.

LODER'S WHITE
arboreum var. *album* x *griffithianum*

LATE APRIL   0°
White   Medium

Delicate pink buds burst into slightly scented, white flowers. The plant is compact, wider than tall, and the leaves are bright green. Vigorous and free-flowering. A top-rated variety. Page I.

LODESTAR
catawbiense var. *abum* x Belle Heller

EARLY MAY   −25°
White   Medium

A David Leach introduction. Large florets with a bold spotted dark green-yellow blotch in a full truss. Exceptionally vigorous plant with superior foliage density.

LORD ROBERTS
Unknown

LATE MAY   −10°
Red   Medium

Give this beauty sun because in shade it becomes leggy and does not flower well. The blooms are dull red, blotched black and the leaves are dark green with a heavy veining. Page III.

LUCKY STRIKE
griersonianum x Countess of Derby

LATE MAY   +10°
Pink   Medium

A sister seedling of 'Anna Rose Whitney' with extremely heavy-textured flowers of deep salmon pink. For best results, it should be grown in partial shade. Page 59.

MADAME CARVALHO
catawbiense hybrid

JUNE   −15°
White   Medium

Similar to 'Gomer Waterer', although smaller. I feel certain you will like its ball-type trusses of white flowers speckled with green. The leaves are a dark green. Page 101.

MADAME DE BRUIN
Prometheus x Doncaster

LATE MAY   −10°
Red   Medium

The bright cerise red flowers are rather thin and need a little protection. The unique pointed leaves of this vigorous plant will also be most attractive in the shade. Page 39.

MADAME FR. J. CHAUVIN
fortunei hybrid

EARLY MAY   −10°
Pink   Tall

The round trusses are formed from flowers which are rosy pink, paler in the throat, and have a small red blotch. Light green leaves are on an upright plant. Page 33 and back cover.

MADAME GUILLEMOT
Unknown

JUNE   −10°
Red   Medium

A fine Dutch hybrid which is a lavish bloomer. You will appreciate the long-lasting, compact trusses of rosy red flowers. A beautiful plant with recurved leaves. Page 68.

MADAME MASSON   LATE MAY   −10°
catawbiense hybrid x *ponticum* var. *album*   White   Medium

Envision a pure white flower with golden-yellow eyes and you will have the picture of this rhododendron. And I know you will enjoy its dark green foliage. Page 33.

MARCHIONESS OF LANSDOWNE   JUNE   −15°
maximum hybrid   Violet   Medium

A prominent, almost black blotch within a pale violet rose flower make this variety truly different. The plant is spreading and rather open. An older, still popular hybrid. Page 107.

MARICEE   EARLY MAY   0°
Selected form *sargentianum*   White   Dwarf

A dwarf, twiggy plant which is very floriferous. The medium green leaves are shiny above and scaly below. Flowers are a creamy white.

MARINUS KOSTER   EARLY MAY   −5°
griffithianum hybrid   Pink   Tall

Similar to 'Betty Wormald'. You will like its pink corolla with brown spotting, dark green shiny leaves and resistance to pests. Upright habit.

MARS   LATE MAY   −10°
griffithianum x unknown parent   Red   Low

The outstanding feature of this variety is the handsome lightly colored stamens, springing from deep true-red flowers. The plant is compact and should have afternoon protection. Page 76.

MARTHA ISAACSON   LATE MAY   +5°
occidentale x Mrs. Donald Graham   White   Medium

This is an azaleodendron hybrid which is very symmetrical and sturdy. Its reddish green leaves adorn the plant all year. Fragrant white flowers are stained pink.

MARY BELLE   EARLY MAY   −10°
Atrier x Dechaem   Yellow   Medium

Excellent plant habit and olive green leaves with a peculiar twist. The long-lasting flowers of heavy substance begin as a coral color in bud, open to a peachy apricot and later turn yellow. Page 106.

MARY FLEMING   EARLY APRIL   −15°
(*racemosum* x *keiskei*) x *keiskei*   Salmon Yellow   Low

A most interesting new, small-leaved variety which is shapely and free-flowering. The blooms are pale yellow with salmon streaks outside the corolla.

MARYKE   LATE MAY   0°
discolor x Fabia   Pink   Medium

A heavy bloomer of large-sized, upright trusses formed from flowers which are a pleasing blend of pink and yellow. Light green foliage and upright plant habit. Of the Van Veen hybrids, I think it is the best for color. Page 56.

MAY DAY   EARLY MAY   +5°
haematodes x *griersonianum*   Red   Low

Intriguing is this plant's tawny indumentum. The foliage is a fine dark green and the bright orange-scarlet flowers are thrilling to behold. Eventually will become broader than it is high.

MEADOWBROOK   LATE MAY   −15°
Mrs. C. S. Sargent x Everestianum   Pink   Medium

Its good hardiness increases its desirability. The fimbriated, deep pink flowers and the foliage are quite good.

MEDUSA EARLY MAY +5°
scyphocalyx x *griersonianum* Orange Low

Certainly an unusual color, a buff orange with patterns of fine vermilion pencilings. The dark green leaves have a light colored indumentum. Dense, compact, rounded plant. Page 111.

MICHAEL WATERER JUNE −15°
ponticum hybrid Red Medium

Rounded, ball-type trusses hold flowers of magenta red. The good, compact plant carries leaves of medium green. Page 23.

MISSION BELLS EARLY MAY −5°
williamsianum x *orbiculare* Pink Low

Slightly fragrant, pale pink flowers in a lax truss dot this tightly-mounded, small-leaved variety. It will take considerable sun exposure. Page 69.

MOONSTONE LATE APRIL −5°
campylocarpum x *williamsianum* Yellow Semi-dwarf

I heartily recommend this as an excellent foliage plant and prolific bloomer. It is seen as a tight mound of oval leaves extending to the ground. Page 85.

MOTHER OF PEARL EARLY MAY 0°
Pink Pearl sport White Medium

There is a faint scent to the shell pink flowers which fade to white. Look more closely for the faint touches of brownish green on the upper lobe. Resembles 'Pink Pearl' in every way except flower color. Page 104 and back cover.

MRS. A. T. DE LA MARE EARLY MAY −10°
Sir Charles Butler x White Pearl White Medium

This variety will delight you with its slightly fragrant white flowers, spotted with green, which are carried in large, dome trusses. Long, dark green leaves on a good plant which takes exposure quite well. Page 66.

MRS. BERNICE BAKER EARLY MAY −5°
Dawn's Delight x *fortunei* Pink Medium

A new and different variety. Pleasing foliage on a plant with somewhat open habit. The flowers, which reflect light very well, have unique markings. Page 79.

MRS. BETTY ROBERTSON EARLY MAY −5°
Mrs. Lindsay Smith x *campyplocarpum* hybrid Yellow Low

The convex, wavy, foliage in a tight plant interests me, and I like the pale yellow flowers with their red centers. Compact, dome-shaped trusses. Page 114.

MRS. C. B. VAN NES LATE APRIL +5°
Princess Juliana x Florence Smith Pink Medium

Starting as rosy buds, the nearly red flowers gradually fade to a light pink, becoming more attractive as they do. Light green leaves. Page 112.

MRS. CHARLES E. PEARSON EARLY MAY −5°
Coombe Royal x Catawbiense Grandiflorum Pink Tall

This handsome plant should be used more frequently. The good, dark green leaves surround pale pink, shaded orchid flowers, speckled with light brown. Page 34.

MRS. CHARLES S. SARGENT LATE MAY −25°
catawbiense hybrid Rose Tall

Certainly one of the finest of the ironclads. Dome-shaped trusses carry compact clusters of carmine-rose flowers which have yellow throats and wavy margins. Page 88.

MRS. DONALD GRAHAM   JUNE   +5°
(Corona x *griersonianum*) x Loderi group   Pink   Medium

     Nine deep salmon pink flowers are carried in flat-topped, open trusses. The upright, open plant has medium green leaves. Another one you will like.

MRS. E. C. STIRLING   EARLY MAY   −5°
griffithianum hybrid   Pink   Tall

     Gardeners of the Southwest like this hybrid. The blush pink flowers are shaded orchid and slightly frilled. Extended, up-curved stamens are very beautiful. Pages 11 and 86.

MRS. FURNIVAL   EARLY MAY   −10°
griffithianum hybrid x *causasicum* hybrid   Pink   Medium

     Wide, funnel-shaped flowers are a lovely pink and enhanced with a sienna blotch. The trusses are dome-shaped and nicely spaced. Attractive foliage on a nearly perfect plant. Page 8 and front cover.

MRS. G. W. LEAK   LATE APRIL   +5°
Coombe Royal x Chevalier Felix de Sauvage   Pink   Tall

     A striking truss of tight flowers with a prominent dark red blotch in the center which spreads to the lighter pink of the petals, giving the blossoms a glowing quality. The leaves are a dull grayish olive green. Pages 26 and 49.

MRS. HORACE FOGG   EARLY MAY   0°
griersonianum x Loderi Venus   Pink   Medium

     Certainly you will love the frosted touches of the medium pink flowers. A nearly red throat enlivens the very large flowers. It withstands full sun. Page 98.

MRS. LINDSAY SMITH   LATE MAY   0°
Duchess of Edinburgh x George Hardy   White   Medium

     A popular variety in California with its white flowers that are slightly spotted red on the upper lobe. Leaves are a light green and plant is upright, open and occasionally pendant.

MRS. LIONEL DE ROTHSCHILD   LATE MAY   0°
Unknown   White   Medium

     Although it is registered as a bright pink, the clone sold in the Northwest has white flowers with a blotch of carmine spots. Truly a fine flower.

MRS. P. DEN OUDEN   EARLY MAY   −15°
Atrosanguineum x Doncaster   Red   Medium

     This variety is quite compact and bears masses of aniline red flowers.

MRS. TOM H. LOWINSKY   JUNE   −10°
griffithianum x White Pearl   White   Medium

     Orchid-shaped flowers open blush, but soon turn to white with a reddish-brown blotch. Very dark green, lustrous leaves adorn a roundish plant. Page 81.

MRS. WM. R. COE   LATE MAY   −5°
fortunei hybrid   Pink   Medium

     A fine Dexter hybrid that has glossy, dark green leaves and crimson-throated flowers of a deep brilliant pink. Large dome-shaped trusses.

NAOMI   EARLY MAY   −10°
Aurora x *fortunei*   Various   Tall

     There are ten clone registered. I would particularly like to draw your attention to 'Naomi Nautilus', 'Naomi Stella Maris', 'Naomi Exbury' and 'Naomi Glow'. All are outstanding with their large, sweet-scented flowers in pastel shades of pink and yellow. Page 63.

NEREID   LATE MAY   0°
neriiflorum x *dichroanthum*   Salmon Orange   Dwarf

     Bell-shaped flowers about an inch wide are in a flat-topped truss. Very compact plant of roundish, dark green leaves.

NESTUCCA   EARLY MAY   −10°

fortunei x *yakusimanum*   White   Semi-dwarf

Named by Cecil C. Smith, this plant has long dark green leaves on a very compact form. Exquisite are the bowl-shaped flowers of white with their brown traces within the throat.

NODDING BELLS   LATE APRIL   −15°

Red *catawbiense* hybrid x *(forestii* var. *repens* x   Red   Dwarf
griersonianum)

A new and novel creation of spreading habit in which the outer branches arch downward, giving the appearance of their reaching out. Open, bell-shaped flowers are a cherry red.

NOVA ZEMBLA   EARLY MAY   −20°

Parsons Grandiflorum x hardy red hybrid   Red   Medium

A good heat-tolerant plant of vigorous, upright growth. It has dark red flowers and foliage similar to 'America' but the plant habit of 'Nova Zembla' is superior. Page 3.

NOYO CHIEF   EARLY MAY   +10°

zeylanicum hybrid   Red   Tall

Truly an outstanding foliage plant. The leaves are parsley-green, highly glossy, and having a plastered fawn tomentum beneath. The tight, bright red trusses add remarkable beauty. Page 29.

OCEANLAKE   EARLY APRIL   −5°

Sapphire x Blue Diamond   Blue   Low

Not as early as other blues, but it flowers longer than the others. You are sure to like the deeper blue color and the delightfully dense array of small leaves.

ODEE WRIGHT   EARLY MAY   −5°

Idealist x Mrs. Betty Robertson   Yellow   Low

Please don't miss this one. It is new and it is beautiful! Glossy leaves cover the compact growth. Profuse flowers of chartreuse to yellow with light carmine speckling in the throat are funnel-shaped and have ruffled lobes. The buds are amber and peach. Pages 75, 126 and back cover.

OLD COPPER   LATE MAY   −5°

Vulcan x Fabia   Copper   Medium

A Van Veen hybrid unique in color and quite aptly named. The handsome, large, bell-shaped flowers hang in a loose truss. Long, dark leaves in a good, upright plant. Page 15.

OLD PORT   EARLY MAY   −15°

catawbiense hybrid   Plum   Tall

Compact, ball-shaped trusses are handsomely covered with deep plum flowers. The medium green leaves cover a vigorous, open-growing plant.

PARSONS GLORIOSUM   LATE MAY   −25°

catawbiense hybrid   Pink   Medium

Re-examine that hardiness factor. This variety can really take the cold, and beautifully, too. The conical truss is made of flowers which are lavender, shaded pink. The leaves are dark green in a compact, upright plant. Page 74.

PEEKABOO   EARLY MAY   0°

(Carmen x Moonstone) x *elliottii*   Red   Dwarf

I like this neat little plant of notable ancestry. It certainly merits your attention. Six-floret trusses carry deep blood red flowers. Rounder foliage is very different. Page 6.

PHYLLIS BALLARD LATE MAY 0°
(neriiflorum x *dichroanthum)* x *discolor* Orange Medium

Lately, there has been a trend toward orange varieties. The color of this one is even more interesting because it is a pink-orange. An attractive plant of long, dark-green leaves with a red petiole.

PILGRIM EARLY MAY 0°
fortunei x Gill's Triumph Pink Tall

You are bound to like the large trusses of rich pink with a few dark markings. A superb plant with fine foliage and upright habit. Page XII.

PINK CAMEO LATE APRIL −20°
Red *catawbiense* hybrid x Boule de Neige Pink Medium

Excellent foliage adorns this sturdy Shammarello hybrid. The flowers are a lovely light flesh-pink illuminated with a pinkish blotch.

PINK FLAIR EARLY MAY −20°
Red *catawbiense* hybrid x Boule de Neige Pink Medium

Bushy growth is produced from an abundance of leathery, dark green foliage. Pastel pink flowers display a conspicuous red blotch.

PINK PEARL EARLY MAY −5°
George Hardy x Broughtonii Pink Tall

Certainly one of the oldest and best known hybrids. A free and open grower with good, light green foliage. The soft pink flowers fade to blush. Pages 43 and 80.

PINK PETTICOATS EARLY MAY −5°
Jan Dekens selfed Pink Tall

As this book is written, the variety has not yet reached the market but will soon. Watch for it. It is exceptional in every way and I know you will want 'Pink Petticoats' in your garden. Page 96.

PINK TWINS LATE MAY −15°
catawbiense x *haematodes* Pink Medium

The light shrimp-pink, hose-in-hose flowers will win you over. They are fleshy and of good substance, with 15 or more florets in each dome-shaped truss. Ovate leaves on a broad shrub. Page 13.

PINNACLE EARLY MAY −20°
Pink *catawbiense* hybrid x Mrs. Charles S. Sargent Pink Medium

Good cold weather plant of fine form and excellent foliage. The cone-shaped trusses are loaded with glowing pink flowers which are highlighted by a delicate citron-yellow blotch. Page 85.

PIONEER EARLY APRIL −20°
Conemaugh x *mucronulatum* Pink Low

An extremely heavy bloomer of a light mauve pink. It is a small-leaved, semi-deciduous Gable hybrid. Page 114.

P.J.M. EARLY APRIL −25°
carolinianum x *dauricum* Lavender-pink Low

A fine new hybrid of compact, bushy growth. The bright lavender-pink flowers are a blanket of beauty in season. Brilliant mahogany-colored foliage is striking in winter, and in spring it becomes glossy green. Sun, shade or drought tolerant. Page 115.

POLAR BEAR JUNE 0°
diaprepes x *auriculatum* White Tall

Could a rhodie so named be anything but white? The green throat is a bonus, as is the flower fragrance. Heavily veined leaves are glaucous below.

PRAECOX   MARCH   −5°
ciliatum x *dauricum*   Lilac   Low

A small-leaved variety which fills out a compact plant. Frilled, rosy-lilac
flowers are bewitchingly displayed in small lax trusses. Page 120.

PRESIDENT LINCOLN   LATE MAY   −25°
catawbiense hybrid   Lavender-pink   Tall

Be sure you distinguish between this one and the red variety called 'Abraham
Lincoln'. Dome-shaped trusses of lavender-pink flowers with a bronze blotch.
It does well anywhere.

PRINCESS ELIZABETH   JUNE   −10°
Bagshot Ruby hybrid   Red   Tall

This 'Bagshot Ruby' hybrid has striking form. Erect and usually asym-
metrical, it sports dark green leaves on reddish, thick shoots. Perfectly shaped
conical trusses hold deep crimson flowers.

PRINCESS JULIANA   LATE APRIL   +5°
griffithianum hybrid   Pink   Tall

Tight trusses of rose-pink flowers which fade to white. A vigorous plant that
will grow as wide as it is tall. Do not over fertilize it. Page 26.

PRIZE   LATE APRIL   −20°
Red *catawbiense* hybrid x Boule de Neige   Pink   Low

A good grower with fine foliage. The delicate shrimp-pink flowers are enhanced by a light yellowish-brown blotch. A very showy plant.

PROFESSOR HUGO DE VRIES   EARLY MAY   −5°
Pink Pearl x Doncaster   Pink   Medium

Looks much like 'Pink Pearl' but the flowers are a little larger and a deeper
pink. The plant habit is less open.

PUGET SOUND   EARLY MAY   −5°
Loderi King George x Van Ness Sensation   Pink   Tall

This hybrid will do well in the Southeast. Its assets are good vigorous
plant habit, dark green leaves, and very large, pink flowers slightly tinged lilac.

PURPLE GEM   EARLY APRIL   −15°
fastigiatum x *carolinianum*   Purple   Dwarf

A cheery little dwarf rhodie with medium green, scaly leaves. Quite similar
to 'Ramapo' with its small trusses of light purple flowers. It does well in full sun.

PURPLE LACE   LATE MAY   −5°
Britannia x Purple Splendour   Purple   Medium

A new variety that very easily fits its name. Compact conical trusses of
purple with lighter centers have exceptionally lacy petals. Plant similar to
'Purple Splendour'. Page 119.

PURPLE SPLENDOUR   LATE MAY   −10°
ponticum hybrid   Purple   Medium

Certainly a very popular variety for the landscape. A compact plant with
dark green leaves with a depressed midrib. The large, ruffled, dark purple
flowers have a black blotch. Page 40.

PURPUREUM ELEGANS   LATE MAY   −25°
catawbiense hybrid   Purple   Tall

Meticulous gardeners like the good plant habit and fine foliage of this hybrid.
Although listed as a purple, the comely flowers are closer to a blue. Page 6.

PURPUREUM GRANDIFLORUM   LATE MAY   −20°
catawbiense hybrid   Purple   Medium

A century-old hybrid of medium purple with a golden-orange blotch. It is
large and handsome, with convex leaves.

PYGMY　　　　　　　　　　　　　　　EARLY MAY　　　　0°
Moonstone x Carmen　　　　　　　　　　　Red　　　　　Dwarf

A dwarf produced from two other dwarfs. It usually grows twice as wide as it is high. The plant is almost completely smothered with the loose trusses of dark red bells.

QUEEN MARY　　　　　　　　　　　　EARLY MAY　　　−10°
Marion x Mrs. Charles S. Sargent　　　　　Pink　　　　Medium

The erect plant is dotted with large rose-colored blooms held in good trusses. Shiny, leathery foliage. Page 38.

RADIUM　　　　　　　　　　　　　　LATE MAY　　　+5°
griersonianum x Earl of Athlone　　　　　Red　　　　　Medium

A variety well-liked in California. The leaves are somewhat shiny and carried upright. The trusses are rather loose and round with flowers of geranium scarlet.

RAINBOW　　　　　　　　　　　　　LATE MAY　　　0°
Hardy hybrid x *griffithianum*　　　　　　Pink　　　　Medium

Carmine-pink flowers with dark edged lobes make this distinctive coloring memorable and apropos to the name. A full plant with shiny long leaves. Page 94.

RAMAPO　　　　　　　　　　　　　EARLY APRIL　　−25°
fastigiatum x *carolinianum*　　　　　　Violet　　　　Dwarf

Wonderful hardiness and the ability to grow in either sun or shade make this one a candidate for the rockery or border. Violet-blue flowers and bluish-green foliage adorn this neat plant. Page 52.

RED HEAD　　　　　　　　　　　　LATE MAY　　　−5°
Atrosanguineum x *griersonianum*　　　　　Red　　　　　Medium

A Joe Gable plant with huge trusses of heavy-textured, bright crimson flowers. Deep green foliage covers this open and spreading plant.

ROBERT ALLISON　　　　　　　　　EARLY JUNE　　−10°
Caroline x *discolor*　　　　　　　　　　Pink　　　　Medium

Another Gable rhodie, rugged and upright in habit with waxy green leaves. Pink, golden-throated flowers are scented. Very floriferous.

ROCKET　　　　　　　　　　　　　LATE APRIL　　−10°
Red *catawbiense* hybrid x Cunningham's White　Pink　　　Medium

Sturdy, upright, dense plant which covers itself with thick, rounded foliage. Deep, radiant, coral-pink flowers are slightly ruffled and blotched with scarlet-red. Page 67.

ROMANY CHAL　　　　　　　　　　JUNE　　　　　0°
Moser's Maroon x *eriogynum*　　　　　　Red　　　　　Medium

You can't help but like the fine round trusses of dark scarlet red flowers and the dark green, recurved leaves. Needs some shade in warmer climates. Page 58.

ROSAMUNDI　　　　　　　　　　　MARCH　　　　−5°
caucasicum hybrid　　　　　　　　　　Pink　　　　Low

An early bloomer which produces strong rose-pink flowers of deeper color than 'Christmas Cheer'. It is slow growing, wide as it is tall. Page 130.

ROSE ELF　　　　　　　　　　　　LATE APRIL　　0°
racemosum x *pemakoense*　　　　　　　White-pink　Dwarf

A graceful, small-leaved dwarf with compact, spreading habit. Heavy-flowering with white blooms flushed blush-pink. Will take full sun but the buds need frost protection. Page 70.

ROSEUM ELEGANS
catambiense hybrid

LATE MAY   −25°
Lavender pink   Tall

A variety popular in the Eastern states and quite successful in the Southeast. Soft rose flowers and medium green leaves are produced by this vigorous plant. Page 105.

ROSEUM SUPERBUM
catawbiense hybrid

LATE MAY   −20°
Pink   Tall

A good purplish-rose for the landscape. Quite similar to 'Roseum Elegans' in plant and flower habit. Page 81.

RUBY BOWMAN
fortunei x Lady Bligh

LATE MAY   0°
Pink   Medium

A superb new hybrid with striking flowers and excellent foliage. Full, domed-shaped trusses of light rose flowers accented by a blood red throat. The glossy leaves with red petioles hold for three years. Page 59.

RUBY HART
(Carmen x Elizabeth) x *elliottii*

EARLY MAY   0°
Red   Dwarf

A new hybrid which blooms profusely with deep, blood-red flowers. Small, dark green foliage. Page 48.

RUTH LYONS
davidsonianum hybrid

EARLY MAY   0°
Pink   Medium

A new and different rhododendron of upright habit. Leaves fold upwards in V-fashion. Flowers of bright pink are carried in open flat-topped trusses.

SAFFRON QUEEN
xanthostephanum x *burmanicum*

LATE APRIL   +20°
Yellow   Medium

This is a sulfur yellow hybrid with funnel-shaped flowers held in lax trusses. An open grower with narrow, glossy, green leaves. Page 123.

SAPPHIRE
Blue Tit x *impeditum*

EARLY APRIL   0°
Blue   Dwarf

Among the finest dwarf blues, it has tiny neat leaves with a slight blue-green cast. The charming flowers are azalea-like with a spicy, aromatic scent you will enjoy. Page 70.

SAPPHO
Unknown

EARLY MAY   −5°
White   Tall

A popular, hardy, vigorous plant clothed with good foliage. Distinguishing purple blotches lay within the white flowers. Pages 25 and 106.

SCARLET WONDER
Essex Scarlet x *forrestii* var. *repens*

LATE APRIL   −10°
Red   Semi-dwarf

I predict that this new hybrid will be rated near the top for flower and plant habit performance. Brilliant scarlet-red flowers of good substance, and nicely-textured, dark glossy green leaves. Page 50.

SCINTILLATION
Dexter hybrid

EARLY MAY   −10°
Pink   Medium

A striking foliage plant, but you should also like the light pink flowers with bronzed throat. Flowers are large and of good substance. Page 32 and front cover.

SEATTLE GOLD
Diva x Lady Bessborough

LATE MAY   0°
Yellow   Medium

A good light yellow with brown markings in a well-built truss. The plant is of tight habit.

SHAM'S JULIET LATE APRIL −20°
Red *catawbiense* hybrid x Boule de Neige Pink Low

A compact grower with showy deep pink buds which open as an apple-blossom pink. The flowers are also enriched with a brown blotch. You will like the good foliage.

SHAM'S RUBY EARLY MAY −20°
America x Red *catawbiense* hybrid Red Medium

Vigorous and conspicuous in the landscape. Dark green leaves are slightly convex. The blood-red flowers are accentuated with a darker red blotch. Juvenile stems are tinged red.

SHOW OFF EARLY APRIL 0°
Moonstone x Carolyn Grace Yellow Low

Gardeners fall in love with the mound of dark green leaves. It blooms with buds tinged pink and light yellow flowers. Very floriferous.

SIR CHARLES LEMON LATE APRIL +10°
Possibly *arboreum* hybrid White Medium

Showy, indumented leaves which are dark green above and deep reddish-brown below. The dome-shaped trusses are faintly speckled in the throat. Page 52.

SNOW LADY EARLY APRIL 0°
leucaspis x *ciliatum* White Semi-dwarf

A compact spreading shrub with small, hairy leaves. Lax trusses of beautiful white flowers with handsome dark anthers. Page 95.

SNOW QUEEN EARLY MAY +5°
White Pearl x Loderi group White Tall

Pure white flowers with a very small red blotch at the base. The large leaves of medium green will not withstand the sun.

SOUVENIR OF W. C. SLOCOCK EARLY MAY −5°
campylocarpum hybrid Yellow Low

Compact trusses bear flowers which open an apricot yellow and fade to pure yellow. Medium green leaves have a twist which is all their own. The plant is upright and compact. Page 14.

SPITFIRE EARLY MAY 0°
griffithianum hybrid Red Medium

One of the Kluis group of fine compact plants. It has deep red flowers with a dark brown blotch.

SPRING DAWN LATE APRIL −20°
Pink *catawbiense* hybrid x Mrs. Charles S. Sargent Pink Tall

Vigorous and bushy, a plant which grows as wide as it does high. The foliage is pea-green and you will enjoy the rosy-pink flowers blotched golden yellow. Page 73.

SPRING GLORY EARLY APRIL −20°
Red *catawbiense* hybrid x Cunningham's White Red Medium

Compact plant with lovely large, shiny foliage. Blooms early with light rosy-pink flowers that have a large crimson-red blotch. Page 84.

SPRING PARADE EARLY MAY −20°
Red *catawbiense* hybrid x Cunningham's White Red Dwarf

Upright and compact plant with small, curved, dark green leaves. Golden scarlet-red best describes the flower coloring. Forces well in the greenhouse for Easter.

SUGAR PLUM   EARLY APRIL   0°
Moonstone x Carolyn Grace   Pink   Low

A dense, upright plant, hybridized by Wright, which has roundish, dark green leaves. I find the wide, funnel-shaped, deep-pink blooms very attractive.

TEMPLE BELLE   EARLY APRIL   −5°
orbiculare x *williamsianum*   Pink   Low

Dainty, bell-like flowers held in lax trusses. Round leaves are light green on a plant which meets the ground.

TESSA   EARLY APRIL   −5°
Praecox x *moupinense*   Pink   Low

An early-bloomer with outward-facing, lilac-pink flowers which open in groups of three to four along the stem at the leaf axils. Small leaves on a good plant.

THE GENERAL   EARLY MAY   −20°
America x *catawbiense* hybrid   Red   Medium

Compact and a nice height for the average landscape. Elegant dark green foliage and good hardiness. The flowers are brilliant crimson red with a dark blotch.

TIDBIT   EARLY MAY   +5°
dichroanthum x *wardii*   Yellow   Low

A feast of beauty with its straw-yellow flowers as they open and shortly turn to a deeper and more intense color. A low grower with dense foliage. Page 95.

TONY   LATE APRIL   −20°
Red *catawbiense* hybrid x Boule de Neige Red   Low

Attractive, slightly crinkled foliage seems made for the bright cherry-red blossoms. The low growth and handsome look assure it a choice spot in the garden. Page 110.

TRILBY   LATE MAY   −10°
griffithianum hybrid   Red   Medium

The gray-green leaves and the flashy red stems are distinctive. The deep crimson flowers are almost black and the darker center spot adds to this effect. Plant is upright and full. Page 103.

UNIQUE   LATE APRIL   0°
campylocarpum hybrid   Yellow   Low

Again the name is fitting. The plant is symmetrical and very compact. Red buds turn to pale yellow, slightly tinged peach, and are carried in a tight mounded truss. Pages 17, 49, 61 and 62.

UNKNOWN WARRIOR   EARLY APRIL   +5°
Queen Wilhelmina x Stanley Davies   Red   Medium

An early rose-red as distinctive as its parents. The leaves are dark green and pointed. Large, dome-shaped truss of about twelve clear red florets. Page 53.

VANESSA PASTEL   LATE MAY   +5°
Soulbut x *griersonianum*   Yellow   Medium

Certainly one of the unusual rhododendrons. Flowers open a brick red, change to apricot, and finally to yellow. Leaves are medium green. Upright.

VAN NES SENSATION   EARLY MAY   −5°
Mrs. Butler x White Pearl   Lilac   Medium

Wide, funnel-shaped flowers of pale lilac with a lighter center. The dome-shaped trusses produce a wonderful pastel effect. Good plant form with *fortunei* type leaves. Page 5.

VAN VEEN   LATE MAY   −5°
griersonianum x Pygmalion   Red   Medium

Rich, clear, dark-red flowers which are enhanced by long, dark green foliage. The open habit can be controlled by prudent shearing. Page VI.

VERNUS   EARLY APRIL   −20°
catawbiense hybrid x Cunningham's White   Pink   Medium

One of the outstanding new hardy hybrids produced by David Leach. An early bright pink with a darker center. Very floriferous in good truss. Good plant habit. Page 46.

VIRGINIA RICHARDS   EARLY MAY   0°
(R. wardii x F. C. Puddle) x Mrs. Betty Robertson Yellow   Medium

A fine compact plant with dark glossy leaves. Ten to twelve florets fill the trusses. The flowers open a pale yellow with pink overcast and turn to a dark yellow with a crimson blotch at the base of the corolla. Page 2.

VULCAN   LATE MAY   −5°
Mars x *griersonianum*   Red   Medium

A very popular variety, and rightly so. It is a compact shrub with dark green, pointed leaves, and heavy trusses with flowers of bright brick red. Page 12.

VULCAN'S FLAME   LATE MAY   −5°
griersonianum x Mars   Red   Medium

The reverse cross of 'Vulcan' and almost identical in every way. Appears to be more heat tolerant. Page 100.

WHEATLEY   EARLY MAY   −15°
Dexter hybrid—parentage unknown   Pink   Medium

One of the finest of the Dexter collection. Large, silver-pink flowers in a good, tall truss. A compact plant with large attractive foliage. Page 109.

WHITE PEARL   EARLY MAY   +5°
griffithianum x *maximum*   White   Tall

A vigorous variety of good form with dark green leaves. Tall, conical trusses of white flushed with slight pink, fading to white. Page 45.

WHITE SWAN   EARLY MAY   0°
decorum x Pink Pearl   White   Tall

A good pure white with a green eye at the base of the upper corolla. The trusses are dome-shaped. The plant is upright and medium compact.

WILGEN'S RUBY   EARLY MAY   −10°
Britannia x John Walter   Red   Medium

I am sure you will like the good trusses which carry bright, deep-red flowers with a dark brown blotch. A proven variety with compact habit and good foliage. Page 125.

WILSONI   JUNE   −10°
carolinianum x *ferrugineum*   Rose   Low

You may find this listed as 'Laetevirens'. An extremely full, small-leaved plant, good for an evergreen background and able to grow in almost any situation. Profuse flowering of small, rose-red blooms.

WINDBEAM   EARLY APRIL   −25°
carolinianum x *racemosum*   Pink   Semi-dwarf

A small-leaved, semi-dwarf that is very popular. I like its highly aromatic foliage and the manner in which the white flowers turn to a soft pink. Page 40.

WYANOKIE   EARLY MAY   −25°
carolinianum x *racemosum*   White   Low

Of good plant habit with dark green lustrous leaves. Very floriferous, with small white blooms held in ball-like trusses.

YELLOW HAMMER

sulfureum x *flavidum*

EARLY APRIL   +10°
Yellow   Medium

I must say that this one is quite different. An upright, open plant with scaly leaves. Very floriferous, it produces small, tubular, exceptionally yellow blooms. Page 30.

ADDITIONAL ILLUSTRATION CAPTIONS

FRONT COVER

A mass planting of 'Scintillation' with 'Blue Ensign' and 'Mrs. Furnival' about to open in the background complement one another very well in this modern garden.

I

LODER'S WHITE, *one of only two varieties which the American Rhododendron Society has rated as superior in both flower and plant habit. The large, slightly scented blooms are pink in bud. The flower buds are hardier than the plant. I have seen 'Loder's White' lose all of its leaves because of freeze damage and yet bloom perfectly.*

II

LAVENDER GIRL, *a delicate color with a suggestion of pink. The flowers are long-lasting. This is a "mauve" variety, the color of the first cheap fast dye invented. It was used by the servants, and thus the implication of "common."*

III

LORD ROBERTS, *certainly worthy of its title. A strong grower which seems to thrive under most any conditions of extreme heat or cold, smog or sun. Try looking at this bloom at twilight.*

IV

Though unnamed, this Dexter seedling stands as a royal sentinel at the garden gate.

VI

VAN VEEN, *I find it hard to understand why my father named this hybrid. He cared little for red, preferring the more delicate colors. Also, he liked variety names which described the character of a plant. Nevertheless, it is a good red and the open habit can be controlled. Does well in the warm areas, but go easy on the fertilizer.*

VIII

AMERICA, *as beautiful as America itself. The best of the hardy reds for flower color. Similar to 'Nova Zembla' which has a more compact habit, but not as pure a red. Grow in sun for better plant development.*

X

ANTOON VAN WELIE, *the golden tip of the pistil points the way to further beauty. A deeper pink than 'Pink Pearl' with a pronounced yellow shading. Heavy foliage which will hold up in full sun.*

XII

PILGRIM, *assuredly worthy of its heritage name. A garden specimen highly prized for its delicate coloring, well-marked foliage, vigorous habit and fragrance of flower. May be grown in sun or shade.*

XII

KING TUT, *trusses form a cross of pink against pea-green foliage. The felted new growth from the parent, R. smirnowii, is an interesting conversation piece. Extremely hardy.*

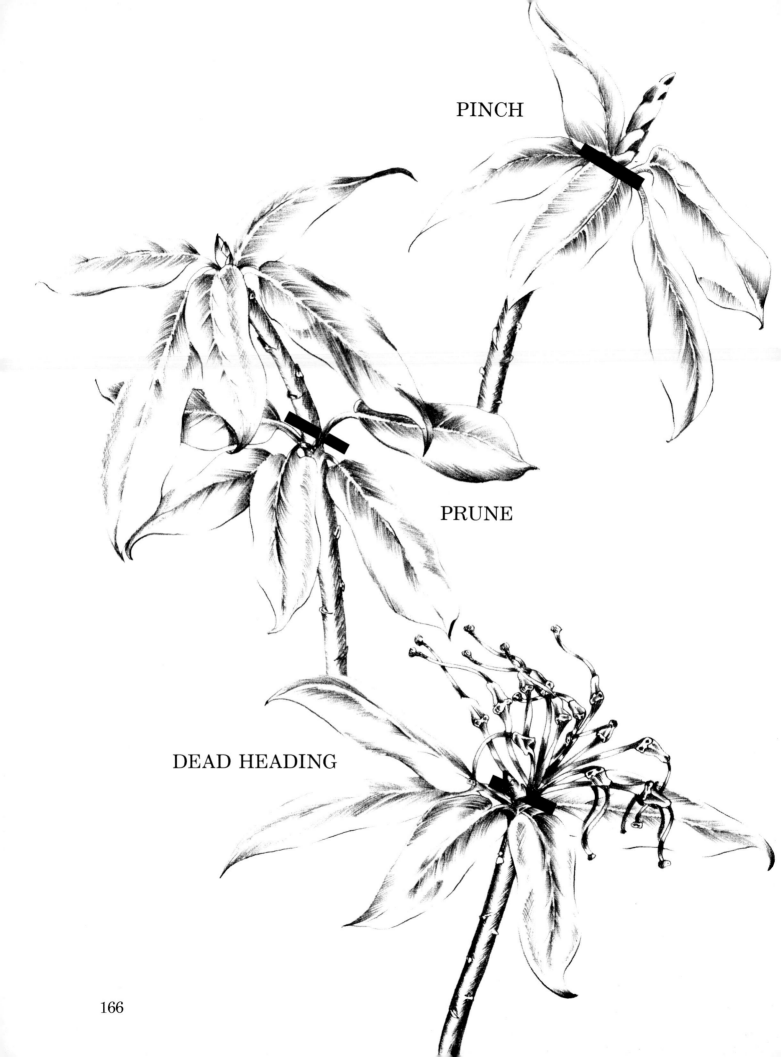

PINCH

PRUNE

DEAD HEADING

166

CHAPTER TWELVE

Rhododendrons Throughout America

Prior to writing this book, I sent survey sheets to a number of friends and experts in rhododendron culture throughout the United States and Canada, asking for information about growing conditions and for advice on growing rhododendrons in their home areas. Here are some of their comments, by location, which I am sure will be interesting to you.

Kentville, Nova Scotia, Canada — "prefer our sandy loams . . . pH in area is 4.5 . . . fairly humid summer weather . . . can be 60 degree temperature variation in 24 hours during January . . . ground freezes to six inches or more for four month period . . . prefer pine needle or sawdust mulch . . . many home owners plant rhododendrons."

Charlotte, North Carolina—"temperature ranges from 4 degrees to 99 degrees Fahrenheit . . . some wind problems . . . pH of 6.5 . . . sulfur used for increasing acidity . . . raised beds and frequent watering important during first two years . . . recommended all Shammarello hybrids, 'Mrs. Furnival' and 'Mrs. Charles Pearson', among others . . . ironclads for beginners . . . high planting . . . good aeration . . . mulching and ample water important."

Hendersonville, North Carolina—"pH 5.0 to 5.5 . . . medium to high humidity . . . quick temperature changes during April and November . . . 'Scintillation' is excellent here

and 'Holden' is one of the best . . . we should start a crusade to get our national and state governments to do some thorough research work on rhododendrons."

Greenville, South Carolina—"wooded areas . . . soil real acid . . . 30 degree temperature variation possible in 24 hours . . . 5-10-10 fertilizer used each year following blooming, liquid iron when leaves are yellow . . . 'America' and 'Crimson Glory' suffer here from dieback . . . 'Blue Peter', 'Cynthia' and 'Parsons Gloriosum'' bloom real well."

West Columbia, South Carolina — "heat may reduce lasting period of blooms . . . find that humus (peat) is best for rhododendrons . . . liberal peat and no fertilizer used when planting . . . lots of watering important in first two years . . . 'Jean Marie de Montague' has been one of the best varieties."

Lisle, Illinois—"plants should be shaded during our winter months, but will stand much light and part sun during the growing season . . . need shelter from strong winds, and good drainage . . . moderate fertilization . . . keep roots cool during growing months . . . 'Dora Amateis' and 'P.J.M.' look good."

Skokie, Ill—"not enough good hybrids are being sold."

Chicago, Illinois — "winter shade is imperative . . . use raised beds on heavy soils."

Indianapolis, Indiana—"dry summers, freeze-and-thaw winters, no snow cover and lots of sun . . . high humidity in June and

July . . . seldom over two to three weeks of frozen soil . . . don't dig holes, but plant on top of ground . . . pH factor must be maintained . . . protection from winter sun is necessary . . . Gable varieties, Shammarello's, and 'Janet Blair'."

Munsing, Michigan — "leaf cutter bee a problem here . . . use a heavy application of 0-20-0 mixed in soil with initial planting . . . stake and tie plants to prevent winter breakage . . . plant where snow will accumulate to protect flower buds and prevent winter burn."

South Euclid, Ohio—"20% Terraclor and 10% Captan in talc at rate of one pound to 100 square feet, disked into soil 6 to 8 inches deep for fungus control . . . once each spring, cotton seed meal, triple superphosphate, sulphate of potash and sulphate of ammonia used."

Tipp City, Ohio—"7.0 pH calls for heavy applications of acid peat moss in soil and use of iron sulphate and ammonium sulphate to lower pH."

Toledo, Ohio—"frost may go from one to three feet into the soil . . . don't mix too much peat into the soil as it holds the frost too late in spring after the sun gets hot . . . the City of Toledo is starting a rhododendron garden."

Huntsville, Alabama — "It is best not to have afternoon shade . . . probably any iron-clad will do all right . . . 'Britannia', 'Elizabeth' and 'David Gable' doing well and blooming."

Warrior, Alabama — "temperatures vary from low of 10 degrees to high of 96 degrees . . . last frost March 25 . . . trees affording high shade mixed with sunlight good . . . don't give rhododendrons much attention once they are established."

Birmingham, Alabama—"use German peat moss, sand in soil . . . beds raised 6 to 8 inches above ground . . . pine needle mulch . . . sun in morning and evening, shade during heat of day . . . 'Anna Rose Whitney', 'Mrs. Betty Robertson' and Shammarello hybrids."

Commerce, Georgia — "plant in straight pine bark . . . 'Vulcan', 'A. Bedford', 'Leo', 'Van Veen' and 'Fabia' bloom easily."

San Antonio, Texas—"raw oak leaves and pecan hulls used for mulch . . . feed with ferrous sulphate every 60 days, ammonium sulphate lightly twice a year, and superphosphate lightly in September . . . water only when wilted in A.M. . . . 'Gomer Waterer', 'Autumn Gold' and 'Belle Heller' best performance."

Huntsville, Texas—"suggest rhododendron trials of varieties in Gulf Coast area, which may be fruitful."

Bellaire, Texas—"have grown them in air-conditioned homes."

Davenport, Iowa—"heavy mulching, use of pine boughs and/or Wilt-Pruf needed after December . . . use heavy watering in fall . . . 11 A.M. to 4 P.M. shade is vital."

Center Point, Iowa — "recommend planting in mixture of soil and sphagnum moss . . . soil should contain some evergreen fertilizer . . . plant where protected from winter sun and afternoon summer sun."

St. Paul, Minnesota—"rhododendrons must be protected with burlap shade during winter . . . 'P.J.M.' comes through with no winter protection."

Madison, Wisconsin—"temperatures range from -30 degrees to 100 degrees . . . use 50% peat when planting . . . acid mulch is absolutely essential, such as oak leaves or pine needles . . . avoid windy areas and keep six-inch mulch on at all times . . . use no manures . . . do not fertilize after June 1 and do not water after August 1 . . . select proper species and varieties."

Ft. Smith, Arkansas—"plant in raised beds, using 50% peat and 50% sand, with good drainage beneath . . . 'Lord Roberts', 'Dr. A. Blok' and Shammarello's."

Florence, Kentucky—"plant in groups in area protected from wind and afternoon sun, with good drainage . . . soil dug out at least 18 inches deep and replaced with mixture of 50% peat moss and 50% top soil . . . use two pounds sulphur per 100 square feet, and cotton seed meal . . . white most popular."

Elsberry, Missouri—"we use ferrous sulphate to counterbalance a build-up of carbonates in our water."

Oklahoma City, Oklahoma—"plant in well-drained soil . . . Dexon used the first year . . . lots of water during growing season . . . in this climate, you must develop a feeling for rhododendrons . . . plant in early fall so plants can harden off and become established before heat and wind in spring . . . plant high . . . provide good air circulation and high shade . . . larger plants establish more easily than those too small . . . 'Antoon van Welie', 'Graf Zeppelin', Mrs. E. C. Stirling' and 'Blue Ensign'."

Concord, Massachusetts—"keep pH at 5.0 to 5.5 . . . water well going into fall . . . mulch with two inches of wood chips."

Burlington, Vermont—"plant in area protected from winter winds by buildings or snow cover."

Monticello, New York—"wood lath shade helps during winter to prevent damage from sun reflecting from snow . . . you must have deer-proof fence . . . locate on grade facing north . . . wind break of evergreen trees is good."

Rochester, New York—"have had trouble with roots of locust trees."

Ithaca, New York — "raised beds of 12 inch pure peat moss to completely insulate roots from natural (alkaline) soil . . . leafy

mulch on top . . . also proved satisfactory in Rochester area and in Edinburgh Botanic Garden."

Trafford, Pennsylvania—"am a strong believer in small amounts of fertilizer often . . . prepare soil at original planting and let nature do the rest, with a little common sense . . . too many rhododendrons die of tender loving care . . . plant on north side of buildings or on east . . . protect against west wind . . . be certain old lime and junk removed from planting area."

University Park, Pennsylvania—"replacement of parent soil with a highly organic soil modified with coarse peat is recommended before planting."

Levittown, Pennsylvania—"heavy soil so plant on top of ground with raised beds . . . use pine needles, peat moss in whole mixture of soil and leafmold . . . wood chips as mulch, but not too deep . . . avoid western exposure . . . 'Albert Close', 'Jean Marie de Montague', 'Mary Fleming' among favorites."

Ambler, Pennsylvania—"am a great bud pincher . . . pine and straw mulches to a good depth are successful . . . like overhead irrigation . . . dwarf rhododendrons increasingly popular in landscape."

Richmond, Virginia—"alkaline city water calls for spring and fall adjustments of pH with iron sulphate . . . generally prefer to leave plants alone and let them grow naturally . . . don't overfertilize . . . plant on top of soil . . . dry cold in winter, drought in summer . . . 5 degree to 100 degree temperature spread . . . use heavy mulch of pine needles or pine bark at all times . . . new growers should start with old hardies . . . use Ferbam for *Phytophthora cactorum*."

Charlottesville, Virginia—"keep well mulched at all times, except in early fall . . . know variety characteristics and hardiness factors . . . plant those which have proven good for the area . . . 46 inches annual rainfall.

Clovis, California—"plant shallow or grow in a solid bed of one-half peat and one-half shavings or sawdust, immediately followed with organic fertilizer before new growth starts . . . depth of planting important."

Compton, California — "hot and dry . . . plant in peat, oak leaf mix . . . provide good drainage . . . acidify soil as needed . . . 'Pink Pearl' and 'Lord Roberts'."

San Rafael, California—"freezing cold and extreme heat . . . humid and windy at times . . . lath cover will prevent windburn . . . overhead sprinkling used to combat high temperatures . . . use raised beds where soil is claylike . . . plant in redwood tubs and use in visual area when in bloom . . . watch moisture factor . . . 'Noyo Chief' is great."

Richland, Washington — "winters usually rather mild . . . hot summers not as much an obstacle as some think . . . planting with a north or east exposure or in other shade almost essential . . . raised beds can be avoided if an acid fertilizer is used . . . my raised beds are composed mostly of horse manure and sawdust . . . mulches are helpful to combat summer heat . . . 'Purple Splendour' among best for this area, takes sun and buds heavily."

One final observation, hybrids with R. *maximum* somewhere in their parentage seem to adapt well to extreme heat conditions. Most of them will require shade, but they do thrive quite well in a warm climate. The following hybrids are worth trying:

Albert Close
Blue River
Broughtonii Aureum
Lady Clementine Mitford
Lady Eleanor Cathcart
Lady Longman
Marchioness of Lansdowne
Mrs. A. T. de La Mare
Mrs. Tom H. Lowinsky
Puget Sound
Snow Queen
Van Nes Sensation
White Pearl

Supplement—1980

Much has happened in the rhododendron world since the first edition of this book was written some eleven years ago. In these new pages I will discuss a few thoughts I've had since that time. As I stated in the opening pages, rhododendrons will be much more widely grown in the future. Their use has extended dramatically, and this is only the beginning.

Many new nurseries are in rhododendron production today, and most of the older ones have greatly increased their propagations. I find these conditions duplicated in Europe, Japan, Australia and New Zealand. The whole world simply has been captivated by the charm of the rhododendron.

Particularly gratifying are sections of America just now showing interest in rhododendrons. Membership in the American Rhododendron Society has increased substantially, with the addition of 15 new Chapters since this book was first published. Also gratifying are the rhododendron display gardens started by many Chapters. Of particular note is the Rhododendron Species Foundation Garden near Tacoma, Washington, the most extensive collection of rhododendron species in this country, which soon will rival any garden in the world.

If I were writing this book today, I would place greater emphasis on the importance of soil conditions and wind protection for better success with rhododendrons. The fine fibrous roots of a rhododendron require oxygen in their growth outward and upward from the rootball. A planting at too great a depth, and soils of heavy texture will snuff out the life of a plant. Yellow leaves and other signs of distress, often blamed on too much or too little fertilizer, alkaline soil, salt damage, or disease, frequently are the result of poor soil aeration.

A soil situation not always understood is the interface problem. By this, I mean the difference between the texture of the soil in what the rhododendron was grown and the composition of the soil in the new planting. An extreme example would be a rootball of heavy clay being planted in sandy soil. All irrigation water would flow through the sand and never penetrate the clay surrounding the roots. As a consequence, the rhododendron will languish and eventually die.

Contrary to general practice, I advocate removal of the rootball wrapping before planting a rhododendron. This will become a very important step in the future as burlap becomes more expensive and less reliably available for the nurseryman. An imitation non-degradable plastic material is replacing burlap. Removal of the wrapping allows the opportunity for hosing away some of the soil to expose the roots for ready contact with the new media in the planting. Container-grown plants should have the tight mat of roots cut and loosened before planting. If the rootball is the least bit dry, be sure to soak it in a tub of water before planting.

Another important phase pertaining to soils is the acceptance of the principle of planting on top of the ground, that is, using raised beds. Soil conditions in the South and Midwest, as well as any other area where drainage is not ideal, would make this concept imperative for successful rhododendron culture.

Shelter from drying winds and excessive direct sunlight is the second most important requisite for a successful rhododendron planting. The evergreen leaves of a rhododendron transpire water vapor continuously night and day, even in subfreezing temperatures. In general, larger leaves will desiccate more profusely and will require more protection. Wind has the effect of increasing the rate of transpiration. A burned leaf is the result of a plant's inability to pump moisture at a sufficient rate from the roots. A cold, dry wind likewise will burn leaves when the ground is frozen.

It seems appropriate to elaborate a bit more about cold hardiness. The American Rhododendron Society publishes hardiness ratings from reports submitted by members residing in all sections of the country. Newer hybrids cannot be rated until sufficient experience with them has been gained. Important is the understanding that these ratings apply to a mature, established plant in good health and with only reasonable protection provided. A newly planted rhododendron is not fully hardy. But more important is the healthy condition of the plant. A good fertilizer and watering program is essential. Insect damage and disease reduce a plant's vigor and ability to withstand cold. Root rot, weevil and nematode damage limit the capacity of a plant to take up full requirements of water and fertilizer. And, don't allow your rhododendron to go into a long winter freeze without plenty of water in the root zone.

As a general rule, rhododendron varieties which do well in the cold climates seem to have the stamina to hold up best in warm environments. Testing of less hardy varieties in recent years has proven the adaptability of many additional hybrids. The use of rhododendrons in the South has increased considerably in recent years.

Since the time this book was written, a number of chemicals have been taken out of production or severely restricted. One new spray I would strongly recommend at this time is Orthene, particularly beneficial in controlling root weevil. This systemic contact spray is quite effective for all sucking and chewing insects. Use as directed by the label. Orthene is not highly toxic and there are no residual effects. Hopefully to solve many of our problems is a new fungicide now being tested. I believe availability and relief is but a short time away.

In 1976, the American Rhododendron Society established a Research Foundation for the express purpose of supporting rhododendron research grants. Studies are now under way on controlling petal blight, identifying beneficial mycorrhizae and understanding cold hardiness. These are worthwhile projects, and as more funds become available other research will be undertaken. A number of years ago the American Rhododendron Society supported a study to develop tissue culture as a means of propagating rhododendrons. This is now a reality and a particular advantage in the ability to quickly increase the availability of new, worthy hybrids.

Rhododendron breeders have produced many exceptional, exciting hybrids in recent years. Early in this book I talked about the potential of new species yet to be discovered in China. The doors are opening once again and plant explorers may soon discover fascinating parents to stimulate the work of the hybridizers.

American Rhododendron Hybrids, published by the American Rhododendron Society, is just off the press. It includes the names of over 1300 registered American hybrids, and many of these are described, at least to some extent. Listed also are another 700 names yet to be registered. Another section names "good doers," a recommended group of exceptional hybrids for each section of the country. For those interested in hybridizing I suggest a close study of Kendall W. Gambrill's article. This is a chart of hybrids by color, size and blooming period. You will notice many gaps in this chart where hybrids are needed, particularly when cold hardiness and heat tolerance are considered.

The following pages include some hybrids not covered earlier in this book. I've grown most of these and believe they merit special listing in this supplement.

My sincere wish is that all rhododendrons will add a new dimension of enjoyment to your life in the same measure as they have to mine.

Hybrids Not Covered Earlier

Airy Fairy	*lutescens* x *mucronulatum* Cornell Pink	Pink	Late March	Low	0°
Alison Johnstone	*concatenans* x *yunnanense*	Pink	Late April	Low	0°
Anna	Norman Gill x Jean Marie de Montagu	Pink	Mid-May	Tall	−5°
Baden-Baden	Essex Scarlet x *forrestii* var. *repens*	Red	Late April	Semi-Dwarf	−15°
Ben Moseley	Dexter hybrid	Lavender	Late May	Medium	−15°
Betty Arrington	Dexter hybrid	Pink	Late May	Medium	−10°
Betty Hume	Dexter hybrid	Pink	Late May	Tall	−10°
Blue Pacific	Purple Splendour x Susan	Blue	Late May	Medium	−10°
Blue Rhapsody	A. Bedford x Purple Splendour	Blue	Late May	Medium	−10°
Bravo	*catawbiense* var. *album* x (*fortunei* x (*arboreum* x *griffithianum*))	Pink	Late April	Tall	−25°
Brickdust	Dido x *williamsianum*	Rose	Early April	Low	0°
Brinny	Day Dream x Margaret Dunn	Yellow	Early May	Medium	0°
Chikor	*chryseum* x *ludlowii*	Yellow	Early May	Dwarf	0°
Conchita	*moupinense* x *ciilicalyx*	Pink	Late March	Semi-Dwarf	+10°
Confection	Corona x Dondis	Rose	Mid-May	Medium	0°
Congo	Goldfort hybrid	Ivory	Early May	Tall	−20°
Coral Velvet	*yakusimanum* selection	Pink	Early May	Low	−10°
Cornell Pink	*mucronulatum* selection	Pink	February	Medium	−25°
Crater Lake	*augustinii* x Bluebird	Blue	Late April	Medium	−5°
Crete	*yakusimanum* x *smirnowii*	White	Late April	Low	−25°
Dame Nellie Melba	*arboreum* x Standishii	Pink	March	Tall	0°
Dolly Madison	*catawbiense* var. *album* x (*fortunei* x (*arboreum* x *griffithianum*))	White	Late April	Medium	−20°
Donna Hardgrove	*fortunei* x (*wardii* x *dichroanthum*)	Pink	Early May	Low	−5°
Duet	*catawbiense* var. *album* x (*dichroanthum* x *griffithianum*) x *auriculatum*	Yellow	Late May	Medium	−20°
Edmond Amateis	*catawbiense* var. *album* x Dexter Sdlg.	White	Early May	Tall	−15°
Epoch	*carolinianum* var. *album* selection	White	Early May	Low	−10°
Etta Burrows	Fusilier x *strigillosum*	Red	Early April	Tall	0°
Exotic	Loderi King George x Ostbo Y3	Red	Early May	Tall	+5°
Fair Lady	*arboreum* var. *roseum* x Loderi Venus	Rose	Early May	Tall	0°
Fawn	*fortunei* x Fabia	Salmon	Early May	Tall	+5°
Fireman Jeff	Jean Marie de Montagu x Grosclaude	Red	Early May	Low	0°
Fred Hamilton	*neriiflorum* x *griersonianum*	Yellow	Late May	Low	−5°
Furnivall's Daughter	Mrs. Furnival hybrid	Pink	Early May	Medium	−10°
Gi-Gi	Dexter hybrid	Red	Late May	Medium	−10°
Golden Star	*fortunei* x *wardii*	Yellow	Late May	Medium	0°
Goldstrike	*oreotrephes* x Royal Flush	Yellow	Early May	Medium	0°
Good News	Britannia x Romany Chal	Red	June	Medium	−5°
Grace Seabrook	Jean Marie de Montagu x *strigillosum*	Red	Early April	Medium	0°
Halfdan Lem	Jean Marie de Montagu x Red Loderi	Red	Early May	Medium	−5°
Hallelujah	Jean Marie de Montagu x Kimberly	Red	Early May	Medium	−5°
Hardijzer Beauty	Kurume Azalea x *racemosum*	Pink	March	Low	−5°
Helen Scott Richey	(*racemosum* x *moupinense*) x *mucronulatum* Cornell Pink	Pink	February	Semi-Dwarf	−5°
Hello Dolly	Fabia x *smirnowii*	Rose	Late April	Medium	0°
Hotei	Goldsworth Orange x (*souliei* x *wardii*)	Yellow	Early May	Medium	−5°
Isabel Pierce	Anna x Lem's Goal	Pink	Mid-May	Medium	−5°
Jade	Fabia x Corona	Pink	Early May	Low	+5°

Name	Parentage	Color	Bloom	Height	Temp
Karin	Britannia x *williamsianum*	Pink	Early April	Low	−5°
Katherine Dalton	*fortunei* x *smirnowii*	Pink	Late May	Medium	−20°
Ken Janeck	*yakusimanum* selection	White	Early May	Low	−10°
Kimberly	*williamsianum* x *fortunei*	Pink	Late April	Low	0°
Lemon Mist	*xanthostephanum* x *leucaspis*	Yellow	March	Semi-Dwarf	+10°
Lem's Cameo	Dido x Anna	Peach	Early May	Medium	0°
Lem's Monarch	Anna x Marinus Koster	Pink	Early May	Tall	−5°
Lori Eichelser	*forrestii* var. *repens* x Bow Bells	Pink	Early April	Semi-Dwarf	0°
Madame Cochet	Parentage unknown	Lilac	Early May	Tall	−5°
Mardi Gras	*yakusimanum* x Vanessa	Pink	Early May	Semi-Dwarf	0°
Markeeta's Prize	Loderi Venus x Anna	Red	Early May	Medium	−5°
Maxine Childers	*strigillosum* x Elizabeth	Red	Early April	Low	−5°
Mi Amor	*lindleyi* x *nuttallii*	White	Late April	Tall	+15°
Minnetonka	Roseum Elegans Seedling	Lavender	Late May	Low	−20°
Mist Maiden	*yakusimanum* selection	White	Late April	Semi-Dwarf	−20°
Moerheim	*impeditum* hybrid	Violet	Late April	Dwarf	−15°
Molly Ann	Elizabeth hybrid	Red	Late April	Semi-Dwarf	0°
Mrs. J. C. Williams	Parentage unknown	White	Mid-May	Medium	−10°
Myrtifolium	*hirsutum* x *minus*	Pink	June	Semi-Dwarf	−15°
Nepal	*wightii* hybrid	White	Early May	Medium	−20°
Noyo Brave	Noyo Chief x *yakusimanum*	Red	Early May	Semi-Dwarf	−10°
Olympic Lady	Loderi King George x *williamsianum*	White	Early April	Low	0°
Parker's Pink	Dexter hybrid	Pink	Late May	Medium	−15°
Party Pink	Mrs. Furnival x *catawbiense* var. *album*	Pink	Mid-May	Medium	−20°
Persia	Mrs. Furnival x *catawbiense* var. *album*	Pink	Early May	Medium	−20°
Polynesian Sunset	Parentage unknown	Orange	Late May	Medium	0°
President Roosevelt	Parentage unknown	Red	Early April	Low	+5°
Prince Camille de Rohan	*caucasicum* hybrid	Pink	Late April	Medium	−10°
Ptarmigan	*leucaspis* x *microleucum*	White	Late April	Dwarf	−5°
Riplet	*forrestii* var. *repens* x Letty Edwards	Salmon	Mid-May	Semi-Dwarf	0°
Roslyn	Purpureum Elegans x Everestianum	Purple	Late May	Medium	−10°
Royal Flush	*cinnabarinum* x *maddenii*	Orange	Early May	Medium	+5°
Royal Purple	Parentage unknown	Purple	Late May	Medium	−15°
Russautinii	*augustinii* x *russatum*	Blue	Late April	Medium	−10°
Serenata	Russell Harmon x (*dichroanthum* x (*discolor* x *campylocarpum*))	Ivory	June	Medium	−20°
Seta	*moupinense* x *spinuliferum*	Pink	March	Low	+5°
Seville	America x Dexter seedling	Pink	Mid-May	Medium	−20°
Shamrock	*keiskei* dwarf x *hanceanum nanum*	Yellow	March	Dwarf	0°
Sham's Candy	Pinnacle x Pink Cameo	Pink	Late May	Medium	−20°
Shanghai	(Mrs. Furnival x *catawbiense* var. *album*) x unnamed seedling	Pink	Late May	Tall	−10°
Skipper	Fawn x Indian Penny	Yellow	Early May	Tall	0°
Snow Cap	*souliei* x (Loderi White Diamond x williamsianum)	White	Early April	Semi-Dwarf	−5°
Spatter Paint	*irroratum* seedling	Pink	March	Tall	+5°
Sweet Sixteen	Parentage unknown	Pink	Mid-May	Tall	−5°
Taurus	Jean Marie de Montagu x *strigillosum*	Red	Early May	Tall	−5°
Thor	Felis x *haematodes*	Red	Early May	Low	0°
Todmorden	Dexter hybrid	Red	Late April	Medium	−10°
Trude Webster	Countess of Derby x unknown	Pink	Early May	Tall	−5°
White Gold	Mrs. J. G. Millais x unknown	White	Early May	Medium	−5°
Whitney's Orange	Parentage unknown	Orange	Early May	Low	0°
Willbrit	Britannia x *williamsianum*	Pink	Early May	Low	−5°
Winsome	Humming Bird x *griersonianum*	Pink	Early May	Low	0°
Wissahickon	Dexter hybrid	Rose	Early May	Medium	−10°
Yukon	*carolinianum* var. *album* x *dauricum* var. *album*	White	March	Low	−20°

Color Illustration Index

Subject Index

HERITAGE NURSERY
5-9-93

JUNE LEES DARK PURPLE
JUNE ABRAHAM LINCOLN (2) RED
JUNE GENIE FARRELL RED
MAY BRAVO (2) PINK
MAY WYNTERSET (3) WHITE
MAY FIREMAN JEFF RED
APRIL SCINTALATION (2) PEACH
MARCH GOOSEANDER (2) YELLOW
APRIL PEEPING TOM (SAPPHO) WHITE c. PURPLE
JUNE DAVID FORSYTHE RED